Readers' Praise for *A Boy's Journey: From Nazi-Occupied Prague to Freedom in America*

Not just another Holocaust book, *A Boy's Journey: From Nazi-Occupied Prague to Freedom in America* by Peter J. Stein grips the reader with heartfelt revelations that can only be expressed by a survivor. The best books on the Holocaust are not only interesting to read but also ask readers to think about their own lives and what they would have done in similar situations. *A Boy's Journey* reminds us to do just that.

Born in Prague two years before the Nazi occupation of Czechoslovakia, Peter Stein spent his early childhood years experiencing the cruelties of Hitler's regime. Stein's book offers an honest, riveting account of life under Nazi rule as seen through the eyes of a child. Readers then experience his transatlantic sailing to America, where he and his mother finally reunite with his father.

So begins his life in a country busy absorbing refugees fleeing war-torn Europe.

The study of the Holocaust is now a required part of school curricula in an increasing number of states across the country. Stein's book should be included in a short list of recommended Holocaust memoirs for students and teachers.

— Sharon Halperin, Director of the Center for Holocaust, Genocide and Human Rights Education of North Carolina

Peter Stein has produced a remarkable tale of Nazi occupation, the Holocaust and emigration that reimagines events from the perspective of a young boy. Part history, part memoir, *A Boy's Journey: From Nazi-Occupied Prague to Freedom in America* is a touching, eloquent act of remembrance.

> — Chad Bryant, author of *Prague in Black: Nazi Rule and Czech Nationalism*

Peter Stein has written a riveting memoir of his experience as a young Jewish boy in Nazi-occupied Prague. Scholars will admire this important contribution to the historical literature of a terrible time, and readers of all ages will find their hearts reach out to the courageous boy who sees one after another member of his family disappear with no plausible explanation. Many, he will eventually learn, die in Auschwitz. And readers will pray with him for the safe return of his beloved father. No one who reads this magnificent book will ever forget the gripping saga.

> — William E. Leuchtenburg, Past President, American Historical Association

Teaching the Holocaust and its implications for today has been my mission in hopes that those who hear us and learn will make a difference. In my judgment reading the book *A Boy's Journey: From Nazi-Occupied Prague to Freedom in America* will generate a lively and insightful discussion of immigration, social justice and democracy.

> — Lynda Moss, Holocaust Educator

A Boy's Journey

From Nazi-Occupied Prague to Freedom in America

Also by Peter J. Stein

Journeys in Sociology: From First Encounters to Fulfilling Retirement (with Rosalyn Benjamin Darling)

Social Gerontology: Issues and Prospects (with Elizabeth W. Markson)

The Essential Sociologist (with Beth B. Hess and Susan Farrell)

Sociology, five editions (with Beth B. Hess and Elizabeth W. Markson)

Single Life: Unmarried Adults in Social Context

Single

The Family: Functions, Conflicts and Symbols (With Judith Richman and Natalie Hannon)

The Marriage Game: Understanding Marital Decision-Making, two editions (With Cathy Greenblat and Norman Washburne)

A Boy's Journey

From Nazi-Occupied Prague
to Freedom in America

Peter J. Stein

LYSTRA BOOKS
& Literary Services

Chapel Hill, North Carolina

A Boy's Journey: From Nazi-Occupied Prague to Freedom in America
Copyright © Peter J. Stein 2019

ISBN 978-0-9996931-2-4 Trade paperback
ISBN 978-0-9996931-3-1 Ebook

Library of Congress Control Number 2018963478

Biography and Autobiography: Personal Memoir

The author can be reached at aboysjourney@gmail.com

Quotation from *Under a Cruel Star: A Life in Prague*, 1941-1968, Heda Margolius Kovaly, 1997, used with permission from Plunkett Lake Press, plunkettlakepress.com/uacs

Unless otherwise credited, all photographs are the property of the author.

Peter J. Stein's biography photo by Gesche Würfel

Book design by Frogtown Bookmaker, frogtownbookmaker.com

Published by Lystra Books & Literary Services, LLC
391 Lystra Estates Drive
Chapel Hill, NC 27517
lystrabooks@gmail.com

LYSTRA BOOKS
& Literary Services

*I dedicate this book to my relatives who were
murdered in the Holocaust:*

*Grandmother, Sophie Markus Stein, Terezin,
Czechoslovakia, August 1942*

*Aunt, Kamilla Stein Bergmanova, Maly Trostinec,
Belarus, September 1942*

*Uncle, Richard Stein, Maly Trostinec,
September 1942*

*Aunt, Karla Stein Waignerova, Auschwitz, Poland,
October 1942*

Uncle, Leo Perutz, Auschwitz, November 1944

Timeline of Historical and Stein Family Events

1932

July 31 — Nazi Party becomes largest party in the Weimar Parliament (*Reichstag*). Hitler gets 37% of vote for President in last democratic election in Germany.

1933

January 30 — President von Hindenburg appoints Hitler as Chancellor of Germany.

April 1 — Nationwide Nazi boycott of Jewish owned businesses.

May 10 — Nazi public burning of books written by Jews and political dissidents.

1934

May 17 — *Victor J. Stein (Jewish) and Zdenka (Helen) Kvetonova (Catholic) marry in Prague City Hall.*

1935

September 15 — The Nuremberg Laws establish the legal framework for persecution of Jews in Germany through anti-Semitic racial theories. Jews are stripped of citizenship and prohibited from marrying or having sex with Aryans.

November 15 — Nazi racial ideology labels persons in "mixed marriages" as *Mischlinge*. Jews are persecuted and alienated in German society.

1936

March 7 — German Army occupies the Rhineland, violating the Versailles Treaty.

1936, cont.

June 17
Heinrich Himmler becomes Reich Leader of the *Schutzstaffel* (the SS), making him the second most powerful man in Nazi Germany.

September 22
Peter Joseph Stein is born in Prague.

October
Paka, Peter's nanny, arrives in Prague from the Sudeten area of Czechoslovakia.

1937

October
Joseph Stein, Peter's Jewish grandfather, dies of cancer.

1938

March 12
Hitler annexes Austria into greater Germany (*Anschluss*); Nazi anti-Semitic laws apply in Austria.

September 23
The Czechoslovak army mobilizes, fearing German invasion of Sudetenland, the borderland region of Bohemia and Moravia, with a German-speaking majority population.

Peter's father, Victor, a First Lieutenant, reports for duty.

September 28-29
Munich Conference: Great Britain and France give in to Hitler's demands; their concessions are called "appeasement."

October 1
German *Wehrmacht* (armed forces) occupies the Sudetenland; Czech Army evacuates without fighting.

November 9-10
Kristallnacht (Night of Broken Glass), an anti-Jewish pogrom takes place in Germany, Austria and the Sudetenland; 200 synagogues are destroyed; 7,500 Jewish shops are looted, 30,000 Jewish men are sent to concentration camps.

1939

January 30
Hitler in *Reichstag* speech threatens "if war erupts it will mean the extermination (*Vernichtung*) of European Jews."

Germany occupies Czechoslovakia.

March
Peter's immediate family witnesses the German occupation, but they do not try to leave Prague.

Some relatives leave for Palestine, England, the Soviet Union and the United States.

September 1
Beginning of World War II: German military attacks Poland; England and France declare war. The wearing of yellow stars by Jews is ordered on September 1, 1941. This law does not apply to Jews married to non-Jews until 1942.

October 12
Nazis begin deportation of Austrian and Czech Jews to ghettos in Poland.

1940

May 10
Germany invades the Netherlands, Belgium, Luxembourg and France.

May 20
A concentration camp is established at Auschwitz.

June 22
Six weeks after Germany attacks western Europe, France surrenders.

July 10
The Battle of Britain begins as the German Air Force (*Luftwaffe*) bombs Great Britain.

November
Jews in Warsaw are herded into a walled-off ghetto. The overcrowded ghetto holds more than 500,000 persons and becomes the largest ghetto in Europe.

1941

June 22   Germany invades the Soviet Union in "Operation Barbarossa."

July 31   Reinhard Heydrich is made head of all security and secret police in the Third Reich. He implements the "Final Solution," the Nazi plan to murder all European Jews.

September 27   Heydrich arrives in Prague to organize the Holocaust and crack down on the Czech resistance.

November 24   First deportation of Czechs to Terezin (*Theresienstadt* in German), a ghetto-labor camp and a holding area for Jews, most of whom were later deported to death camps. Terrible overcrowding, oppressive living conditions and disease led to the deaths of more than 33,000 persons there.

December 7   Japanese Air Force attacks Pearl Harbor.

December 11   United States declares war on Japan and Germany.

1942

January 1   First deportation from Terezin to "the East," to camps in Eastern Europe especially Riga, Lublin, Treblinka and Auschwitz.

January 20   Heydrich convenes the Wannsee Conference "the Final Solution of the Jewish problem....an organized plan for the massacre of all European Jews." (Wistrich 2001). The Wannsee Conference marked the beginning of the Nazis' official plan to systematically kill all European Jews.

iv

1942, cont.

May-June Heydrich, called the Butcher of Prague by the Czechs, is shot by Czechoslovak parachutists on May 27, 1942. Nazi terror follows, including the total destruction of the towns of Lidice and Ležáky.

Summer-Fall

Peter's grandmother, Sophie Marcus Stein, is sent to Terezin, where she dies in 19 days.

Peter's uncle, Richard Stein, and his wife, Elsa, are sent to Terezin and to Maly Trostinec extermination camp in the Ukraine (now Belarus) and murdered.

Peter's aunt, Karla Stein Weigner, and her husband, Rudolph, are sent to Terezin and then Auschwitz, in Poland, where they are murdered.

Peter's aunt, Kamilla Stein Bergman, her husband, Richard, and their son, Erich, are sent to Terezin and then to Maly Trostinec, where they are murdered.

Peter's father, Victor Stein, is ordered to perform manual labor (slave labor) in various areas of the Protectorate of Bohemia-Moravia.

1943

July 1942- February 1943 The Battle of Stalingrad is a turning point in the war, as the 6th German Army of over 1 million soldiers loses to the Soviet army; almost 100,000 German soldiers surrender.

Capt. Kurt Fanta, Peter's cousin, and his wife, Capt. Malvinka Fanta serve with the 1st Czechoslovak Army Corp, fighting alongside the Soviet army against the German army.

1944

The SS deport about 90,000 Jews from Terezin to death camps Auschwitz, Majdanek and Treblinka. In 1944, Nazis beautify the ghetto and stage a propaganda film titled "Hitler Gives the Jews a Town." (USHMM. 2018. "Theresienstadt: Red Cross Visit.").

November

Last train taking Jews to death camps leaves Terezin. Leo Perutz, Peter's uncle, is sent to Auschwitz, where he is murdered.

November-January

Prisoners from concentration camps such as Auschwitz are forced to evacuate to Germany. The "death marches" result in many deaths.

With thousands of other prisoners Peter's cousins Jan and Tomas Marcus and Mana Arendt and daughter Sonja are forced to march during the terribly cold winter of 1944.

1945

Winter-Spring

Peter's father is sent to Terezin.

The postwar Czechoslovak Government (Third Republic) is established in April 1945.

April 30

Hitler commits suicide.

V-E Day: Germany surrenders; end of the Third Reich.

May 5-9

Prague Uprising begins as Czech resistance fighters and citizens battle German Army units in the streets. Soviet army enters Prague, May 9th.

May 9

Peter's father returns from Terezin on a Soviet Army truck. The family is reunited.

May or June

Peter's nanny and companion, Paka, is rounded up with other German-speakers from the Sudeten and shipped to Germany. Peter never hears from her again.

vi

1945, cont.

May 26	In the first post-war election in Czechoslovakia, the Communist Party gets 38% of the vote. Edvard Benes becomes President and Klement Gottwald, a leader of the Czech Communist Party, becomes Prime Minister.
September 2	Japan surrenders; end of World War II.

1946-1948

Peter's parents make numerous trips to the American Embassy in Prague to secure American visas.

1948

February 25	Communist coup occurs; with support of the Soviet government, the Czech Communist Party overthrows the democratically elected government; President Benes resigns on October 5.
October	*Peter and his parents board a train from Prague to the Czech border, where his father must exit because he does not have an American visa. Peter and his mother Helen continue the trip to Dresden, Amsterdam and Rotterdam, where they board a steamship.*
November 8	*SS Amsterdam sails into New York Harbor with Peter and Helen aboard. That evening Harry Truman is re-elected president of the United States.*
November	*Peter and his mother move to Larchmont, New York where she becomes a governess and Peter starts the sixth grade at Murray Avenue Grammar School.*

1948-1952

In April 1951, Peter's father, Victor, arrives in New York. He finds work in Manhattan. Peter continues his schooling in Larchmont. He graduates from Mamaroneck Junior High in 1952. The family is reunited in New York City.

Czechoslovakia Prior to the German Invasion, 1939

Table of Contents

Life Remembered in Photographs:
Prologue through Chapter 17

Part II: Life After World War II, 1945-1948

Part III: Life in America, 1948-1952

Life Remembered in Photographs:
Chapters 18 through 38

Prologue

A knock on the door startled me. It was the fall of 1993, and I was in my college office, reviewing lecture notes for the day. When I opened the door, I didn't recognize any of the four students standing there. One young woman was crying, and the other woman and two men looked angry. I motioned for them to come into my office and asked what happened. Their answers came out in a torrent of words:

"Professor Stein? Can we talk to you? In our Social Problems class, the sociology professor questioned how many Jews died."

The student showed me a handout written by the professor: "The media theme that 6 million Jews died in concentration camps has since 1990 been dropped to about 1.5 million. Given the technical questions surrounding air photos and the transportation and crematoria capacity, a figure between 700,000 to 800,000 appears more realistic."

The young man's voice broke. The professor apparently said that the blockade by the British and American armies was responsible for most of the deaths in the camps. The Germans did not have enough food for themselves, so they could not feed the Jews, and it wasn't Germany's fault.

I was stunned.

"Did any of you challenge him?" I asked.

"He wouldn't let us speak or ask him anything."

I knew the professor they were talking about was a fan of Joseph Stalin, dictator of the Soviet Union, and Benito Mussolini, dictator of Fascist Italy. He had their photos in his office and he even organized a "Day of Appreciation for Mussolini" on our college campus. He had written a book praising East Germany, which had officially been called the German Democratic Republic, but in reality was a communist state allied with the Soviet Union during the Cold War.

Now it seemed that my colleague was also a Holocaust denier. I wanted to know more. Apparently what happened was that Professor X told his class that films and television distort the truth. His example was Stephen Spielberg's 1993 film *Schindler's List,* which had just been released. Oskar Schindler was a German industrialist who saved the lives of more than 1,000 Jewish men and women by employing them in his factories. The professor said the film was mostly fiction, an assertion that made all four students angry. One student said she could not believe what she was hearing. Her grandmother, the only member of a large Jewish family to survive the Holocaust, had miraculously endured Auschwitz. Over the years, she had told her granddaughter about the horrors of that place. When the student tried to tell the professor about her grandmother, he cut her off, saying hers was only one person's story, that he needed much more data before making a conclusion.

The four students, all of them Jewish, were so distressed they all spoke at once. They were concerned that some students in the class might not realize their professor was distorting the truth. They asked what it would take to get him fired for lying to students.

I reassured them that the Holocaust had indeed happened and that 6 million Jewish men, women and children and another 5 million others were killed by the Nazis and their collaborators. I also mentioned the extensive evidence and scholarship documenting the atrocities of the Holocaust. I suggested looking at information at the United States Holocaust Memorial Museum in Washington, D.C. And then I told them about my own relatives who were murdered and about my father who, like the student's grandmother, survived.

Another student wanted to know why the professor did not let them speak. He asked whether academic freedom applied only to faculty but not to students. I said that academic freedom is supposed to protect the right of professors to express their views on topics in which they are experts. Then I added that academic freedom should also protect students' rights to challenge professors, and they certainly should not be penalized for questioning a professor's views. Academic freedom does not mean professors can ridicule students or impose their own personal or political views. A college classroom should be a safe place to express ideas.

In a few minutes I found a quote from U.S. Supreme Court Justice William O. Douglas: "The most important aspect of freedom of speech is freedom to learn.... Education is a continuous dialogue—questions and answers that pursue every problem on the horizon. That is the essence of academic freedom, of all scientific inquiry."

I did not mention my initial impression that their professor, who was a tenured member of my department, sounded like a Holocaust denier: a person who believes the Holocaust never happened or wasn't so extensive, who questions how many Jews were killed and who distorts history.

The students asked me to come to their class to "set the record straight." I said I would try.

About a week later, with the professor's consent, the head of my department and I went to his Social Problems classroom. The professor was not in class that day. We covered the major historical and political developments leading to the Holocaust and showed a clip of a French documentary film, *Night and Fog*, to help students understand the concentration camps. From their comments, I sensed the students began to understand the extent and horror of the Holocaust. When we finished our presentation, they had a lot of questions.

That disturbing day in the fall of 1993 changed the direction of my personal and academic life. The incident with the students upset me deeply, and I realized I had a responsibility to act. I needed and wanted to learn more about the Holocaust, its victims and perpetrators, and about my own family's experiences.

Most of all I wanted to have a long conversation with my father, but he was no longer alive. I wished we had had many more conversations about his experiences and the tragedies he faced in the deaths of his mother and his siblings. I also wanted to understand how he and some other relatives survived. I reread his letters and documents, and I managed to contact several relatives who survived the Holocaust, especially cousin Vera Marcus Novak, 10 years older than I, who as of this writing lives in Kingston, Canada. She is the informal family historian and knew my Jewish grandparents well. I am also grateful to my cousin, Gertrude Perutz Stalev, only four years my senior, with whom I grew up in Prague during the war. She now lives in Clayton, North Carolina. Both were generous with their time, insights and encouragement, and from photographs they helped to identify relatives I had never met. I also used my research skills and my own remembered experiences to understand what happened to our extended family.

The next semester I began to teach classes on genocide and the Holocaust with two colleagues who have researched and written about the Holocaust: biologist Myriam Wahrman and psychologist Neil Kressel. Our class included annual trips to Ellis Island, the Museum of Jewish Heritage in downtown Manhattan and presentations by various Holocaust survivors. With a group of dedicated faculty members, we started a Center for the Study of Genocide and the Holocaust, developing many educational programs, workshops and lectures for our public university and the community in northern New Jersey. With support from Dr. Paul Winkler, executive director of the NJ Commission on Holocaust Education, we organized workshops for educators teaching genocide and the Holocaust to students in middle schools, high schools and colleges.

Years after the encounter with the Holocaust denier, my wife and I moved from New York to Chapel Hill, NC, where I worked as a sociologist at the Institute on Aging at the University of North Carolina. During that time I met two dedicated and energetic second-generation survivors, called 2Gs, Sharon Halperin and Debbie Long. I became active in the Center for Holocaust, Genocide and Human Rights Education which provides speakers for schools, colleges and universities, local organizations and public events. And we videotaped the very moving stories of survivors to preserve their memories for future generations, available on the website holocaustspeakersbureau.org.

Since 2007, when we moved to Chapel Hill, I have spoken at least 80 times to middle school, high school, college and university students and staff and various professional groups.

The North Carolina Council on the Holocaust, chaired by Michael Abramson, selected me as the state's Holocaust Scholar from 2014 through 2016. I organized and ran workshops for teachers across the state with Professor Lynda Moss. I also participated in a number of seminars and workshops to more fully understand genocides and audited a memorable class on the History of the Holocaust taught by UNC-Chapel Hill Professor Christopher Browning, a prolific Holocaust scholar and author of *Ordinary Men* and *Remembering Survival: Inside a Nazi Slave-Labor Camp*.

I was 12 years old when I left Prague and did not return until I was 30. I've been back with college friend Victor Rosenzweig, with my dad and with my wife, Michele, our son, Mike, and his wife, Sarah. I revisited familiar places in Prague and Braník, an area about 20 minutes from downtown, where I lived with my parents during and after World War II and also Terezín, called *Theresienstadt* in German, a ghetto and concentration camp outside of Prague. The Czech language started to come back to me and all kinds of memories, pleasant and difficult, flooded my brain.

Honoring my relatives' memory is important for me. I do this, as long as I'm able, by devoting my time and energy to spreading the lessons of the Holocaust through teaching and running workshops for young and old. I get pleasure from trying to answer the many questions of students and adults, such as "Were there food shortages during the war?" "Why did American and British planes fly over Prague?" "How did you feel during the war?" and "How did your father, mother and you survive the Holocaust?" During one presentation, I showed a photo of Adolph Hitler and the Nazi flag in my Prague classroom. When a student asked me what I told Hitler when I met him, I had to reassure the students that I had never met Hitler in person, but I did see his photos virtually every day.

Part I

Life under the Nazi Occupation and the Holocaust

1936-1945

Chapter 1
Disappearances

When my father disappeared the first time, I was too young to remember, but I imagine I sat on the Oriental rug in my parents' apartment playing with my favorite stuffed toy, a bear. My father probably wore the uniform of a first lieutenant in the Czechoslovak Army, green-gray with a silver bar. Most likely, he picked me up, gave me a kiss and stroked my hair. Then he embraced my mother and headed off to a central gathering place for Czech army reservists.

It was September 22, 1938, also my second birthday, when the Czech army was mobilized. The Czech government, anticipating an invasion by the German army, sent Czech army reservists to the Sudeten, the northwestern area of Czechoslovakia, to defend the country. Most of the people living in the Sudeten spoke German but were Czechoslovak citizens. The local Sudeten German Party became a major pro-Nazi force in Czechoslovakia aiming to break up the country and join the Third Reich. Hitler used the pretext of protecting the Sudeten Germans to eventually invade Czechoslovakia.

Increasingly, Jewish families living in the Sudetenland were harassed. Jewish children were prevented from going to school. Businesses were vandalized and some were seized. My family was directly affected when the German army occupied the Sudetenland in October 1938. Aunt Kamila, my father's sister, her husband, Emanuel Bergmann, and their son, Erich, lived in the Sudeten area. Emanuel owned a textile factory that was looted during *Kristallnacht* in November 1938, and he decided to quickly move his family to safety in Prague. Tragically, safety disappeared four months later, when Prague itself was occupied by German troops. In the fall of 1942, the Bergmann family was sent to their deaths in Maly Trostinec.

I must have missed my father and been puzzled by his absence, but he returned home from the Sudeten area in less than a week. The Czech army was prepared to fight, but there were only a few skirmishes with the German army and war did not materialize. Without being consulted the Czech government was told that the British and French governments signed a treaty with the German government, known as the Munich Agreement which allowed Germany to annex the Sudetenland.

Most Czechs viewed the Munich Agreement as a "sellout" to Hitler. Although Neville Chamberlain, the prime minister of England, declared that the agreement would bring "peace in our time," it did not happen. Winston Churchill, the future prime minister of Great Britain, prophetically declared, "Britain and France had to choose between war and dishonor. They chose dishonor. They will have war." World War II started less than a year later. The Munich Agreement is now regarded as a failed act of appeasement to Germany.

In the earlier years of the war, when I was between the ages of three and six, my father left home several times and returned some weeks later. When I asked about him, my mother would say that he was on a business trip traveling around the country. She usually ended with "He'll be back soon," or "He'll be back as soon as he can." When I was younger, I fully believed my mother, but when I started school at the age of six I became more skeptical. When I pressed her and wanted more details, she would not say anything more. And when I asked about my favorite uncle, Richard, who also went missing from time to time, I got the same answer: he, too, was traveling and would be back when possible.

Then in 1944, when I was eight years old, Dad came into my bedroom, gave me a hug, and told me to listen to my mother and to be a good boy. On his coat was a yellow six-sided star, upon which, in black letters, was printed the word *Jude* (Jew). Then he left, and this time he did not return. He disappeared. For the rest of the war, my mother was a single parent, having to survive and raise me alone. She must have been worried about what was happening to her husband and what would happen to us. I don't know if she confided her worries to anyone; perhaps she told her parents or her sister, but she might have kept everything inside. That was my mother's style, keeping silent about her worries and fears.

My father was my pal, and I missed him very much. I wanted to be with him and wondered why he didn't take me along on these business trips. I remember feeling lonely and wishing I had a sister or a brother to play with. My cousin Robert, who was my age, had a sister, so why couldn't I? The disappearance of other relatives—Uncle Richard, Grandmother Sophie and other aunts and uncles—increased my loneliness and confusion. I wanted everyone to come back even though I had no idea where they were or what was happening to them.

My toys continued to give me pleasure. By now, stuffed animals had been replaced with painted metal toy soldiers—English, American, Czech—and American Indians. Many of these action figures were gifts from Uncle Richard, who himself had disappeared when I was six. If I was well-behaved, a "good boy," my mother rewarded me with new soldiers. I believe my mother wanted to make my childhood as normal as possible. She helped me set up battle dioramas so that when my father and Richard returned, I could show them the war scenes.

As World War II advanced, the only toy soldiers available in the local store were German. For several years, I set up battles between German soldiers (bad guys) on the one side and American, Czech and British soldiers (good guys) on the other. The patterned rug on the floor of my room was my favorite place to stage battles.

If the good guys found themselves overmatched by the Germans, who had more and stronger weapons, I'd have the Indians attack the Germans. I learned from a book that Indians specialized in unexpected attacks, so I sprang them loose when the Germans least expected it. Sometime the Indians attacked a convoy of trucks from the sides or from behind, or blew up a bridge carrying supplies to the frontline Germans. The Indians were the fiercest of all fighters and had no fear.

Prague, where we lived, has been described as the "golden city," a place of mystery and discovery, triumphs and tragedy. Fewer than six months after the Munich Agreement, the German army marched into Prague. The Nazis split Czechoslovakia into two countries: the Protectorate of Bohemia and Moravia and the Slovak Republic. Both areas were controlled by Hitler's Germany. What the Nazis called a "protectorate" was really an occupied country. There was no protection for Czechs, and the Jewish community was to be destroyed.

At age six I began school, and it was then that I really started to notice German soldiers. I saw soldiers every day and everywhere—in the street, on trams, in stores, on trucks and drinking beer at the outdoor beer garden near our home. They wore green-gray uniforms and often carried rifles, revolvers, backpacks, folded shovels and sometimes even canisters with gas masks. At first they seemed like my toys coming to life, and I wondered why my mother was afraid of them.

When I first started to ride the street tram to school, I noticed that the soldiers' uniforms were neatly pressed and their faces looked serious and ready for a fight. As the war intensified and continued, the German soldiers I saw in the streets and near our home looked more tired. Some returning from the warfront showed injuries: a bandaged shoulder, arm or hands. At least once, I saw a soldier using crutches as he walked. I wanted to look more closely, but my mother had warned me not to look at any soldiers and I felt that staring was a bad idea. I remember feeling shocked. Toward the end of the war, the soldiers were either considerably older—a few looked like my grandfather—or a lot younger, probably only a few years older than I.

Shortly after the occupation the German army built a truck depot in our neighborhood. A number of trucks and a detachment of soldiers were stationed there, and a high wooden fence prevented civilians from looking in. But we could see movement in and out of the depot. For me, my parents and the neighbors, the depot and activity around it were constant reminders of the German occupation and the presence of soldiers.

The soldiers I most dreaded were the Gestapo, husky men recognizable in full-length dark leather coats patrolling the streets and seeming to observe everyone. I heard the grown-ups whisper that the Gestapo could arrest anyone, anytime, on a hunch or just because they wanted to. My grandfather told me that innocent persons had no recourse to a hearing or a trial; they just became the victims. I didn't really understand, but I knew to be afraid.

I was a scared boy throughout those war years. I often wanted to look over my shoulder to see if anyone was following me. My stomach was tight much of the time, and I learned to keep my eyes down and my mouth closed. My mother said it was safer that way, not to call attention to myself, to blend in.

A few times I told my school friends Edvard and Daniel that I was afraid and they had similar feelings. We did not know what would happen next. When we heard a rumor about a German defeat, we felt better. To be safe, I had to go straight home from school. My mother controlled most of my activities.

But disappearances scared me the most. My father's mother—my Jewish grandmother, Sophie—and my aunts and uncles all vanished without saying goodbye. I never got an explanation about where they were. Most family get-togethers stopped. We still had weekend visits with my mother's sister Olga and cousins Gerti and Robert, but Leo, their Jewish father, was not seen. I was told that he, like my father, was on a business trip. But Leo never returned. He was killed in Auschwitz in 1944. My father's siblings also never returned.

As a child I did not know these disappearances were due to my relatives' religion. Many years later, as an adult, I learned about the Nazi plan to eliminate all Jewish men, women and children because they were Jewish. That, in itself, was sufficient.

Chapter 2
Courting in Prague

When I was a child, my two older cousins, Vera and Gerti, told me the story of how my parents met. In the spring of 1932, my mother was walking from her parents' home to the tram station. My father was driving his old convertible car in the same direction and offered her a lift. She accepted. He had seen her before near her father's lumber mill, and she had seen his car on the road, often speeding. They had a lively conversation during the drive and discovered that they both liked popular music. Soon they started dancing regularly at a dance hall in Prague on Sunday afternoons.

They fell in love and on a sunny day in May 1934, 31-year-old Victor Stein, who was Jewish, married 30-year-old Helen Kvetonova, a Catholic, not in a synagogue or church but in the Old Town Hall in the middle of Prague. My mother liked to show me her favorite photo, taken as they left the building. She wore a knee-length wool crêpe dress and carried a bouquet of red roses. He wore a three-piece suit topped off with a bowler hat. They were beaming. I was born about two years later.

Prague, an ancient city, had become the capital of Czechoslovakia, a Central European nation established in 1918 after the end of World War I. Prague was the home of cultural, artistic, musical, literary and architectural activities, attracting visitors and tourists from all over Europe. As with many other large cities, it was also a place where Catholic, Protestant and Jewish men and women met, dated and married. My parents were one of those couples. Although my father's father had been very active in a synagogue in Kolín and my father had a bar mitzvah at age 13, he attended synagogue infrequently as an adult, mostly on high holidays. My mother was baptized as an infant and had her Catholic confirmation at age 12, but she also attended church infrequently, mostly on Easter and Christmas, and their marriage had been a civil ceremony.

But religion would become central to their experiences a few years after their wedding. The Nazi Party was gaining power in Germany in the 1920s and by 1933 Adolph Hitler became Chancellor of Germany; the harassment of Jews and opposition politicians began and increased. Many Czechs were hopeful that there would be no encroachment on the independence of Czechoslovakia, but Germany invaded Czechoslovakia in March 1939 and World War II began six months later, on September 1, 1939.

My father graduated university with a background in engineering and business and, when he was 30 years old, opened a bentwood manufacturing factory. It was located about five miles outside of Prague near the Vltava River. The factory manufactured a number of items made from bentwood—rocking chairs, cribs, high chairs for babies and toddlers, tennis and ping-pong rackets, skis and even wooden suitcases. He was very proud that in the 1930s, several top Czech and French tennis players competed with his Standard Brand rackets. Standard meant a desirable level of quality.

My mother was also a college graduate. She spoke French fluently and spent two years near Paris teaching French preschoolers. She was active and enjoying hiking, swimming and skiing, but one day at age 25 or 26 she suffered an injury that set limits on what she could do. She had been crossing a street in downtown Prague when she was struck by a young man on a bicycle. He was trying to make time through busy traffic, and as he changed lanes he swerved into my mother. The impact of the bicycle fractured her leg, and she was rushed to a hospital for surgery. Unfortunately her leg was not set properly, and my mother had a noticeable limp throughout her life. She refused a second operation that might have corrected her limp because she did not trust the doctors. But my mother lived a full life, determined not to become handicapped by her injury. She continued to be physically active and pursued activities she had done before the accident. Later in life she utilized a sturdy umbrella and still later a cane to help her walk. She continually pushed herself and never complained about her situation or condition. Her lesson for me was not to quit and not to feel sorry for myself.

When I was born in 1936, my parents lived in an apartment house in a section called Braník, a few miles from downtown Prague. There was one apartment on each of the four floors of the building where we lived. The front door of our third-floor apartment opened into a foyer, where we hung our jackets and overcoats and left our shoes. The foyer held a pot-bellied coal stove that heated most of the apartment, although it was always much warmer in the foyer than in any other room. As I remember it, one door led to a large living room with a piano, which my mother often played. The dining area held six comfortable chairs and my favorite piece of furniture, a red leather sofa, where I liked to play with my stuffed animals and, later, read the daily newspaper. The sofa sat at the far end of the living room, near a set of windows that faced the street and, in the distance, the Vltava River.

My parents' bedroom was to the left and my smaller one was next to theirs. Most of the photos of the apartment I've seen were taken in the bedrooms, most of them of my mother holding a bundled infant, me. In the back of the apartment were a kitchen and another small bedroom, where Paka slept.

Paka was our housekeeper, my nanny, from the time I was born and my companion throughout the war. She seemed like a second mother, especially after the Nazi occupation, when my mother was forced to work in a textile factory during the day and some evenings. Paka took me to school, picked me up after school, took me to the local playground, clothed and fed me and comforted me when I was ill.

There was a tram stop near the front of our house. The No. 21 train went to downtown Prague in one direction and toward my father's factory in the other. The city of Prague had an extensive network of streetcars that provided transportation for most people.

Across the street from our home was a playground with one area for small children and a large field where, especially on weekends, the neighborhood kids played football. On some Sunday afternoons the field was used by a local team in an organized football league.

When it was too cold or wet to go outside, my mother let me ride a red tricycle around the apartment. I made up an imaginary bicycle track, not unlike the one I saw in a photograph, with lots of turns and twists and a straight runway where I could pedal fast. It was great fun and I got plenty of exercise. But one day, when I was five or six, my father returned home earlier than expected and was startled to see me racing around the apartment. When he noticed that I had chipped off a piece of an elegant wooden chair, he became angry and yelled at me. I got off the tricycle quickly, ran to my room and started to cry. I became scared when he yelled. I did not like him when he did that.

My father read a daily newspaper, magazines and history books, and he liked to exercise and play football and tennis. My mother preferred fiction and books about travel and art. She was an excellent cook and baker and had a pile of cookbooks in the kitchen. She also liked to look at photos of faraway places: Alaska, Africa, wildlife around the globe, beautiful scenery. She had an artist's eye. She enjoyed lively colors and painted still life pictures of flowers, fruits and landscapes. She had studied painting in Prague and was influenced by visits to museums there and later in Paris, where she especially loved to look at French Impressionists. I still have several of her paintings.

I had two sets of grandparents. Joseph and Sophie Stein were my father's parents. They were Jewish. Antonín and Zdenka Kveton, my mother's parents, were

Catholics. Antonín and Zdenka were very important in my life and helped us survive during the Nazi occupation.

My mother, Helen, and her sister, Olga, were raised as Catholics, but as adults their church attendance was irregular. Their father also seldom went to church, mostly on major holidays such as Easter and Christmas. As young women, the two sisters led active social lives, and their friends included both Christians and Jews. Their Jewish friends were assimilated, meaning they identified themselves primarily as Czechs, university students and young professionals and less as Jews. They practiced their Jewish religion but mixed with Christians. Before World War II, Jews made up about 15 percent of Prague's population and about 5 percent of the total population of Czechoslovakia.

It was not surprising that Olga, my mother's younger sister, met Leo Perutz, a successful Jewish businessman, through a mutual friend. They shared common interests, fell in love and married in December 1931. A few years later my mother, Helen, met and married Victor Stein, also a successful Jewish businessman. Both Olga's and Helen's weddings occurred in civil ceremonies in Prague's ornate Old Town Hall, officiated by a justice of the court.

Following my parents' ceremony, they celebrated at her parents' house with food made by her mother. My cousin says that my mother wouldn't have wanted anything elaborate, so an at-home celebration was just fine.

I've often wondered how my Catholic grandparents, the parents of two eligible young women, responded to the fact that both of their daughters chose Jewish men. Were they pleased, or would they have preferred husbands who were Catholics? My cousin Gerti said that although my grandparents were not pleased at first, they adjusted to it. Apparently, Grandmother Zdenka was a determined matchmaker, but the one time she arranged for an afternoon tea to introduce my mother to a Catholic gentleman who owned a jewelry store, my mother never showed up for the event.

It turns out that Leo Perutz's mother, Marie, had also hoped that her Jewish son would marry a nice Czech Jewish girl, and she was not happy with Olga. Yet when Olga was invited to the Perutz home, she made such a good impression that Marie relented. I am told that in the end both grandmothers, Catholic and Jewish, got along well and grew to like one another.

Because her younger sister's marriage was working, the religious ice had been broken. Her Catholic parents had no serious objections when my mother announced that she too wanted to marry a Jewish man. It seems that Sophie, my father's mother, would have preferred a Jewish girl, but she came to like my mother, and their wedding plans were blessed by both sets of parents. More recently, I discovered that marriages between Jews and Christians in Prague in the 1920s and 1930s were not unusual. Mixed marriages between Jews and non-Jews—once a rarity—had increased to about 31 percent by 1933. (Brot, Čapková and Frankel 2010)

Everything changed before my third birthday. My grandfather, Joseph, died. My parents and other relatives seemed more worried and anxious, and there were more hushed conversations between adults. My parents stopped listening to the radio when I was around.

Chapter 3
Czech Army Mobilization

I have a black and white photo of my father in a Czech army uniform displaying the bars of a first lieutenant. Another young man in a sergeant's uniform stands next to him. They look serious and perhaps worried about their next assignment as army reservists. The photo was probably taken in 1938, when German generals amassed troops along the border, forcing the Czech government to mobilize its armed forces. This threat led to a massive call-up of Czech army reserves and a hasty recruitment of young men into the army. On September 23 1938, Czech forces called the Czech Armada, which included my father's division, were moved into the Sudetenland.

As an adult, I've seen documentaries of reservists boarding trucks, trains, tanks and airplanes to travel north to the Czech-German border. There were images of parents, wives, children and girlfriends hugging their men goodbye and weeping. The newsreels show Czech soldiers in good spirits waving goodbye to crowds. Were they really glad to be mobilized, or were those smiles hiding their fears?

The military question facing Czech political leaders and army generals was whether their country of 7 million could successfully fight a country of 70 million. Although the Czech army had modern weapons and an extensive system of fortifications along the Czech-German border, they probably could not match German firepower. Yet Czech soldiers—the army and air force—were determined to put up a good fight.

As I look at the photos of my father in uniform, I wonder how my father and mother coped with a possible war with Germany. How did they react when my father got the orders to report for duty? What did they say to each other? What was left unsaid? What did he pack? And how did his mother and siblings react, since he was the only person in the family in the army? His brother and uncles were too old to serve; he was the only one of military age.

Did he pick me up and hug me before he left? Did he wish me a happy birthday, since this happened right around my second birthday? Was he feeling brave or scared? And, when he reported to his military base, what did he, as first lieutenant, tell his troops? Hitler was flexing Germany's military muscle by insisting that a section of Czechoslovakia be controlled by Germany. The Sudetenland was home to about 3 million German-speaking Czech citizens, and the area was important to Czechoslovakia because most of its border defenses were located there, as were many of its banks and heavy industries. The Sudeten German Party was ordered by Hitler to agitate for their independence, which he later used as an excuse to invade.

I was too young to understand what was happening, but I'm told there was a lot of anxiety in the streets and homes of Prague. Great Britain and France had signed a mutual defense treaty with Czechoslovakia earlier, but in 1938 the British and French governments refused to send their troops to aid the Czechs. The mobilization of Czechoslovak troops ended when the Munich Agreement, signed on September 29, allowed Nazi Germany to annex those portions of Czechoslovakia called the Sudetenland. Czechoslovakia considered itself betrayed by England and France.

The Munich Agreement had turned over to Nazi Germany more than one-half of Czechoslovakia's coal and a substantial proportion of its iron, steel and electrical power. The Sudetenland also had a high concentration of industries such as textiles, glass works, papermaking and toymaking. Without those resources, the Czechoslovak nation was vulnerable to complete German domination.

When German troops occupied the Sudeten, local Nazis and Czechoslovak Germans rejoiced, but most Czechs wept. Czechoslovakia was carved up, ending its 20-year democracy.

Czech reservists returned home within a week but were frustrated because they wanted to fight. My father strongly objected to the "Munich giveaway," yet he feared that, had the Czechs fought, they would have lost badly and much of the country would have been destroyed. Most Czechs, including my parents, resumed their pre-occupation lives. My father went back to managing his bentwood factory, and my mother split her time between taking care of me and working in my father's office. Paka helped maintain my life: playing at a nearby park, playing at home and visiting a few relatives. She was good about keeping life "normal." I was busy, amused and well-fed. I'm sure I felt the tension around me, but I did not have the words to express it.

In March 1939, five months after the Munich Agreement, German troops marched into Prague. The Czech army did not fire a shot. Six months later, in September 1939, Hitler invaded Poland and the Second World War began. Everyday life changed with the German invasion. German became the official language. There were German soldiers and Nazi Gestapo agents everywhere. There was less and less freedom. I don't know what my parents told each other privately, but I learned much later that they considered sending Paka and me to safety in Switzerland. That never happened.

The puzzle of why more Jewish families did not leave when they had a chance has been an overriding question for those of us who survived the war and had relatives die at the hands of the Nazis. Many Jews and Christians read or knew about Hitler's book *Mein Kampf* (My Struggle), in which he lays out his dream of conquering Europe and destroying the Jewish population. There were news reports about German militarization, and visitors to Germany in the 1930s witnessed the military buildup. The bellicose speeches of Hitler, Goebbels and others, hailing the advances of National Socialism and criticizing communists, socialists and Jews, were broadcast on the radio and shown in news films regularly.

In November 1938, during *Kristallnacht* (the Night of Broken Glass), most synagogues in Germany, Austria and the Sudetenland were burned to the ground, Jewish-owned stores were looted, and about 30,000 Jewish men were arrested. At the time, some Jewish families recognized the beginning of Nazi oppression and left Germany and Austria. Other Jewish families believed life would return to normal and they would survive. The Western press covered these events, but many, like *The New York Times*, placed such stories inside their papers rather than on the front page, where they would have received more attention. (Lipstadt 1993)

While some Jewish families left Germany, Austria and Czechoslovakia in 1938 and 1939, tragically, too many stayed. At that time it was difficult for most Jewish families to obtain visas. After September 1, 1939, it became almost impossible. Western countries closed their borders to almost all refugees, and by the fall of 1941 people could not get out.

My cousin Gerti Perutz Stalev, four years older than I, expressed the complications in trying to leave. Her Jewish father, Leo Perutz, became concerned in 1938 that Germany might invade Czechoslovakia. He sent his family to safety on a train to Romania to stay with other relatives. Gerti remembers a long train ride, welcoming relatives and then an unexpected phone call from her father saying that the Munich Agreement had been signed and there would not be a war. The family returned to Prague, assuming that they would be safe because Leo's textile business was needed by the Nazis; this would protect their lives.

My father had a similar response. Before the war, he had German customers for his bentwood products. He spoke German, visited Berlin on business and fully believed that life would normalize. Many years later, when my parents and I lived in New York City, I asked my father why he and other members of his family did not leave. His reasoning was similar to that of many Jewish families. He knew that Hitler and the Nazis were dangerous and they threatened to harm Jews, but he did not expect the horror of the Holocaust. He and other relatives lived comfortable lives, owned homes and property and had funds in banks. All his siblings spoke German fluently and had friends in Germany and Austria. He was concerned about the Nazi threat but believed his family could survive even if life became more difficult. Every member of the Stein family remained in Prague.

But the situation increasingly worsened, and life became unbearable. The Nazis created numerous obstacles. There were food shortages, the news was censored and oppressive laws were enacted. Jews were harassed and sent to ghettos and concentration camps. As with so many other families, mine was trapped in Prague.

Chapter 4
Life in Occupied Prague:
German Soldiers and Allied Bombings

It was a Monday morning in 1943, and the sky was still dark. My father was away on a business trip some-where; Mother never told me where he might be. She woke me up with a gentle tug on the blanket. It was time for me, a seven-year-old second-grader, to get up for school. She helped me dress quickly to avoid the cold of the unheated apartment. I put on my underwear, a shirt, woolen trousers, a heavy sweater and boots she helped me lace up. Before the war our entire apartment had plenty of heat in all the rooms. But as the war dragged on, there were increasing coal shortages and less and less heat. Mother lit the stove only for part of each day and extinguished the flame at night.

In the kitchen my mother heated up what she called coffee and buttered a piece of day-old bread. When I took a sip of the hot beverage, it had a bitter taste. She reminded me that we were drinking chicory, a root that people roasted and drank because of coffee shortages. "That's all we have," she said. She herself had been used to drinking tasty coffee in France before the war, but she was a realist.

My mother and I walked to the nearby street tram stop to get to my school in central Prague. She kissed me as I hopped on the tram and spotted an empty seat. I pulled a school book from my knapsack and began to read. In the knapsack were several other books, sharpened pencils, an eraser and a shiny red apple for a morning snack. I would have preferred candy but knew there was a shortage of sugar. Mother also liked sweets, and on Sundays she treated me to ice cream or baked a cake that would stretch for much of the week.

It was about 7:00 in the morning, and with each stop more people got on, until the tram was crowded. I read for a while until I noticed a soldier in front of me. I first saw his black polished boots, then a dark blue-gray uniform and, as I looked up, his clean-shaven face. He wore a cap with skull and crossbones on the brim and, above that, a flying eagle. My friends and I knew about the several different units of the German army, and I realized immediately that he was a member of the dreaded SS (an abbreviation for *Schutzstaffel*). He looked large, and when he shouted the words "*Steh Auf-gib mir dein platz*" (Get up and give me your seat), I panicked. I stuffed everything into my knapsack, got up, said "*traurig*" (I'm sorry) and moved quickly, shaking, to the other end of the car. My head was spinning. Would he follow me to school? Did he know where I lived? Did he know where my father was? And did he know that I was partly Jewish?

By the time I started school, I knew that being Jewish was a problem. My mother warned me not to tell anyone that I was partly Jewish. When I questioned her, she said, "You might get into trouble." A couple of my school friends also had one Jewish parent, and we might have talked about what that meant. There may have been other warnings from my grandparents, and I probably overheard some radio broadcasts, perhaps part of a speech by Hitler, assailing Jews.

The tram finally reached my stop at the bottom of Vaclavské Namestí (Wenceslaw Square), in the main part of Prague. As I got off, I looked around to see if the Nazi officer was following me. I did not see him, and I felt my chest unknot as I headed across the street to school. It was a four-story building nestled among other gray buildings in a shopping area not far from the main square, the national theater and the opera house. Still shaken, I looked around before entering the building. I walked up a flight of stairs to my second-grade homeroom.

Ms. Novak, my teacher, usually greeted her students as they walked into our classroom. She spotted me right away. I must have looked upset, with my red eyes and pale face. She asked what had happened, and I told her the whole story, sniffling as I spoke. She assured me that the officer only wanted my seat and that he did not know who I was or anything about my father. My body was stiff with fear, but her hug made me feel better.

Ms. Novak knew a lot about her students' families. She had met my parents, and she knew my father was Jewish and my mother was Catholic. There were other kids in the school from mixed religious marriages. But we almost never discussed politics. We all knew that was entirely too dangerous.

My mother continually warned me to be careful and not to mention my Jewish father in public. "Stay out of trouble" was her mantra. But, as in many schools, our class had a bully. His name was Jakub. He was one of the biggest and strongest boys in my grade. Once, in the hallway between classes, the boys were talking about military uniforms, and Jakub said he liked what German soldiers wore. I wondered why he seemed to know so much about German army uniforms and why he admired their military victories. My friends and I thought Hitler was funny-looking, an opinion we only whispered. One day, Jakub overheard us and said Hitler was a great leader and we shouldn't make fun of him. When I told my mother, she told me to stay clear of Jakub. But he had begun to pick on me. He liked to bump into people, especially on the stairs.

A couple of times, he tried to push me down the stairs. I tried to get away from him but he kept badgering me. One day it got worse. "Hey Stein, you're a dirty Jew." I had had enough, so I grabbed him and started to pull him down. I threw the first punch, but he blocked it and then hit my nose. I tried hitting him back, but my nose started to bleed. Our male teacher broke up the fight and took us down to the principal's office. All the way, Jakub kept taunting me. I felt bad for not putting up a better fight and letting my dad down. After a brief lecture from the principal, we returned to class, where we were told to sit on opposite sides of the room.

When I got home my mother was upset by the caked blood around my nose and cleaned it. Then she scolded me for getting into a fight. "I told you to stay out of trouble." But she also said something that helped me understand Jakub. "Jakub's parents do not like Jews and their son is the same." That opened my eyes, and I promised to stay away from him.

At school we saw pictures and posters of Hitler every day as we sat in our desks facing the front of the room; each desk was bolted to the floor. There were two flags above the blackboard. One was a white, red and blue flag, representing *Reichsprotektorat Böhmen und Mähren* (the Protectorate of Bohemia and Moravia). The other was the flag of Nazi Germany, which had a red background, a white disk and a black *Hakenreuz* (swastika) in the middle. Between the flags were two photographs: Adolph Hitler wearing a military uniform and a stern expression, and Emil Hácha, the Czech president of occupied Bohemia-Moravia. He wore a gray suit and a blank expression.

Despite the war and occupation, our teachers tried to cheer us up. The walls were covered with colored charts and photographs: rivers, trees and budding flowers, country scenes with snow and spring flowers. Our two teachers taught us mathematics, reading and writing, biology and the Czech and German languages. Mr. Prochaska, somewhat older and a ringer for our president, was enthusiastic about science and math, which he taught with lots of energy. He seemed less interested when he taught German. He answered our questions about German by saying, "It's in the grammar book and you can look it up." There were also maps of occupied Europe, and our teachers sometimes spoke about the "glorious victories" of the German army. We didn't think they believed what they said, and we sensed that they were ordered to tell us that Germany was winning the war.

I learned that some so-called German victories were lies because on many Sundays I listened to the real news on the wireless radio with my Catholic grandfather. On Mondays, in school, my friends and I quietly exchanged the latest war news, even though our parents told us not say anything.

Chapter 5
The War Looms Closer to Home

Nineteen forty-four was the sixth year of the war, and I was an eight-year-old in the third grade. I didn't know it at the time, but my father had been forced to do hard labor for some time before being sent to a concentration camp. This labor included heavy physical work such as moving heavy material, repairing roads, shoveling and digging.

In the earlier years of the war, we heard about Nazi victories on the radio, in newsreel films and from our teachers, but by 1944 the fighting came closer to Prague. We heard air-raid sirens with greater frequency, and we saw more German soldiers and military supplies on the streets. Some soldiers were being shipped to battles, while others came back from the front.

In late 1944 and early 1945, the American, British and Canadian air forces flew over Prague with increased frequency. Most of the bombers flew around and sometimes over Prague to drop their bombs on Germany. A few Allied flights were aimed at the munitions plants and factories on the outskirts of Prague.

Sometimes air-raid warning sirens went off during our school days and forced the teachers to take us to the school's basement. I knew the drill: quickly stuff all books and papers in your desk; put on your coat and cap; assemble in the back of the classroom; walk quickly and quietly to the basement shelter.

As soon as I heard the low wail of the sirens, a haunting sound that announced a possible bomb attack, my fear started. A couple of times my body started to shake. We did not know the target, and I always hoped Prague would not be it. I reasoned that because we were innocent victims we should not be bombed. The Germans were the bad guys.

We reached the school basement in a few minutes. It was a dimly lit, unpleasant space with a small number of benches. The teachers sat on the benches while we, the third-graders, sat on our coats on the bare concrete floor. Daniel, Edvard and I sat together. We listened to the engines of the planes, wondering if they were American or British bombers. Edvard insisted that he could tell the difference from the sound of the engines. "If it's a Rolls-Royce engine, it purrs." I told him he was making that up, but he seemed confident.

We would wait a while in the basement, until we heard the all-clear siren and returned upstairs to our classroom. The clear signal indicated that the allied bombers were headed for Germany and we were safe. My friends and I got used to it and agreed that today's good news was that we might not have our afternoon German class.

On February 14, 1945, the wailing sirens announced the day's air raid and we moved quickly. The teachers were upset as they hurried us to the basement. We heard loud explosions, much louder than ever before. By the time we reached the basement, one loud crash followed another. Prague was being bombed, and I was scared. There were more explosions, then an eerie silence, followed by louder and stronger explosions. Some students started to cry and I felt numb, clenching my fists and biting my lips, trying not to cry.

Then we heard the sounds of fire engines, followed by ambulance sirens. The sounds came in continuing waves. Daniel whispered that the bombs must have landed close by. We wondered what had been hit: military targets, civilian targets, our homes? Our school was located in downtown Prague with no military targets, so why were we bombed? I suddenly thought about my mother and started to worry about the factory where she worked. Could it have been hit?

My friends and I did not know any of the details of the bombing while hiding in the school's basement. We heard the bombs exploding, along with the wailing sounds of an alarm, followed by the sounds of fire engines and ambulances racing to neighboring bombing scenes near the center of Prague. Everyone in the basement seemed scared, both the students and our teachers.

When we finally heard the all-clear signal, we returned to our classroom, where our teachers tried to comfort us. There was a long wait until most parents arrived and it gave Edvard, Daniel and me time to speculate about the bombing. We all agreed that the end of the war was closer than the German authorities were telling us and that the Allies were winning the war.

In fact, this bombing was meant for Dresden in Germany. Three waves of about 1,300 Allied bombers attacked Dresden in two days, mostly British Lancaster bombers and American B-17 Flying Fortresses. They dropped about 3,300 tons of bombs on the German men, women, and children. The devastation to Dresden was so complete that even today the estimates of people killed vary between 35,000 and 135,000.

At the time of the attack, we did not know that those threatening bombs were American. Years later I learned that a squadron of American planes hit Prague because of a "navigation error." The American pilots thought they were over Dresden in Germany instead of Prague, partly because the topography of Dresden was similar to that of Prague.

During the attack forty American B-17 bombers dropped 152 tons of bombs on central Prague killing more than 700 persons and wounding more than 1,000. All those who died were civilians. More than 300 houses and historical sites were destroyed, yet no Nazi-controlled factory was damaged.

After the bombing, the Nazis spread propaganda claiming that the bombing meant the Americans and British were really enemies of the Czech people. Radio broadcasts and newspapers asked why true friends would bomb us. Yet for Czechs and my grandparents, the bombing signaled that the war was not going well for the Germans. The Allies had landed in Normandy; the Russians were sweeping westward toward Germany; and British, American and Canadian planes were increasingly bombing Germany; the German Luftwaffe had lost most of its planes.

A second bombing one month later was planned to target the industrial area which included factories in northeastern Prague across the Vltava River from our house. Three waves of more than 500 planes pummeled the area at night for about an hour and a half destroying factories and munitions plants and killing about 370 persons. That night I awoke to loud blasts and saw a stream of yellow, red and gray smoke coming from the other side of the river. I jumped out of bed and got close to a large window to stare at the wave of bright lights. There were loud explosions as the window started to shake. It was all eerily strange, watching the flames across the river in the distance. I heard rat-a-tat, rat-a-tat, rat-a-tat and saw traces of white bullets streaming from the ground up to the sky. These must have been German anti-aircraft guns attacking the bombers.

My mother rushed into my room and grabbed my arm. "Get away from the window." We rushed to the kitchen on the other side of the apartment, away from the river and bombing of the munitions plant. I clutched her hand as the blasts continued to light up the sky, and the scary noise continued. Finally, there was silence. And then we heard the wailing sirens of fire engines and ambulances racing to the bombed area across the river.

My cousins Gerti and Robert lived on that side of the river. I asked my mother whether they were safe, and she reassured me that their home was not near the targets and that they would be fine. She made me feel better by saying that the bombing was a sign that the Allies were getting closer to Prague. For me, Americans getting closer to Prague meant that my dad would come back sooner.

I knew my mother worried about my father, but she did not talk about him much. She never told me where he was. If he was indeed traveling for business, I wondered why her face looked so stern, her mouth so tight, and why she had deep lines on her forehead. I tried not to think about him during the week when school and homework kept me busy. But on weekends I really missed him and our time together exploring the neighborhood, meeting people or going to the river.

To add to my anxiety about the presence of German soldiers, a scary story spread around our school. Kids repeated a rumor that some strange men were going around Prague, climbing into people's chimneys and kidnapping children. No one saw the kidnappers' faces, because they were covered in black from the soot in the chimneys.

But Karel, the most skeptical of our friends, nixed all of the speculation. He argued that such men could not fit into the narrow old-fashioned chimneys, and could not carry children up or down a chimney. "Don't believe it," he insisted. But most of us were still scared. When I asked my mother about the kidnappings, she also said it was a made-up story. And anyway, she said, "We have no chimney in our apartment." But just in case, we made sure we locked the front door every night.

I learned about the war and bombings from the Sunday afternoon radio broadcasts of the *British Broadcasting Corporation* (BBC) news from London, which my cousin Robert and I listened to with our Catholic grandfather. Listening to foreign broadcasts on the radio was illegal and punishable by arrest or even death. My grandfather listened anyway, upsetting my mother because we all could have been arrested if a neighbor had reported us.

But Grandfather downplayed any danger and said that all the neighbors were also listening to the BBC.

I was an impatient eight-year-old trying to understand what was going on. I can't imagine how many times I asked two questions: "When will the war end?" and "When will I see my father again?" My grandfather usually stroked my hair and reassured Robert and me that the war would be over soon and we'd see our fathers again.

Chapter 6
My Other Mother, Paka

Paka was my second mother. I was only a few days old when, in the fall of 1936, she came to live with us in Prague. She was a Czechoslovak citizen who spoke very little Czech, a language she never mastered. She spoke only German because she grew up in the Sudetenland where most people did not speak Czech.

I never knew her real name. How did she become Paka? My mother said that when I tried to pronounce her real name, it sounded like Paka, so that became her name. Apparently, she did not mind. Sometime later I also learned that there were few jobs for her in the Sudeten, and she preferred to live in a larger city like Prague. She had lived in Prague before, when she was a governess for Erich, the infant son of my father's sister, Kamila, and so my parents hired her.

Paka enjoyed music and art and visited galleries on her day off. She got along well with my mother, who also loved music and art. Mother spoke German fluently so communication between the two women was no problem. Paka was similar in stature to my mother. Both were of medium height and slim and enjoyed outdoor walking. Several times strangers mistook them for sisters. Both preferred darker colors in clothes, the plainer the better, and neither used much makeup.

Paka could dribble a soccer ball and was also an accomplished ice skater. In the absence of neighborhood friends, she was often my playmate. Like my mother, she was a quiet woman and seldom raised her voice. Although slim, she was quite strong and was able to help me up three flights of stairs in our apartment house when I injured my leg. She was able to carry bags of groceries for blocks and then up the stairs to our apartment. I have no memory of her ever being ill.

But communication around our neighborhood was a problem, because Paka's command of Czech was poor, and during the Nazi occupation neighbors and merchants resented her speaking the language of the occupiers. I was with her one day when she tried to place an order with the local butcher. In a brusque tone, he said that he could not understand her Czech. When Paka repeated her request in German, he would not acknowlege her. She became angry and grabbed my hand. We stormed out of the store. On another day, she had a similar experience with the local baker.

My mother asked both shop owners to be more cooperative, but they were unhappy that a Czech family would employ a German nanny during the Nazi occupation. My mother explained that Paka was legally a Czech citizen who was a well-qualified caretaker, but the Czech merchants did not care. In their eyes, Paka was the enemy, even though she opposed the Nazi Party and was not interested in politics. They labeled her a dirty German.

I remember another encounter, when Paka and I were sitting in a street car returning from school. I was reviewing my German homework with Paka and a few passengers overheard us. Suddenly a Czech woman walked up to us and in an angry voice asked Paka why she, a German, was taking care of a Czech boy. The woman wanted to know where we lived, but Paka refused to tell her. We were both upset and got off at the next stop and walked home. I was unhappy. Did the woman know who we were? Why did she attack Paka? Would she bother us again?

Both my mother and Paka were cautious and deliberate in what they did. Both watched the weather, and I was often overdressed when they sent me outside bundled up. From them I learned to be careful, not to take risks and to protect myself. I think that's why I liked sports so much. I could assert myself without their supervision and take risks on a soccer field or on ice.

Throughout the German occupation my mother warned me never to tell anyone that my father was Jewish, to stay away from political discussions and not to say anything critical about Hitler and the Nazis. These early lessons in being cautious have stayed with me throughout my life.

When my mother—along with other Christian women married to Jews—was ordered to work in a factory making clothing for the German army, Paka's help became even more important. Paka became my second mother. She enjoyed the outdoors and liked to walk, so when we had time, we'd walk rather than take the tram. She had a lot to say about nature but not much to say about people. When flowers started to bloom, she said, "They'll soon show their red and blue colors." She grew up on a farm and seemed attuned to changes in the weather; she knew when fall was coming or when a gray sky would bring snow. She also knew when the current in the river where I swam was strong and I needed to be extra careful. I don't think she spent much time with anyone outside our family, nor did she mention the parents, siblings or friends she left behind. It seemed normal to me that my companionship was all she needed.

One day after the war ended in the spring of 1945, it was my mother, not Paka, who waited for me in front of the school. I wanted to know what happened. My mother said Paka had gotten a call about her father, who was ill, and she had to rush back to her home to see him. Mother tried to reassure me that Paka sent her love and promised to come back soon, but I was inconsolable and acted like a spoiled kid. "I want to see her now," I shouted. I kicked at the ground. Why did she leave me?

Years later, I realized that my mother was protecting me from an ugly political truth. At the end of the war, the new Czech government and many Czech citizens wanted revenge. The Sudeten Czechs who lived in Prague, like Paka, were considered enemies. They were harassed and rounded up and deported back to Germany. As many as 500,000 women, men and children were expelled from Czechoslovakia in the spring and summer of 1945.

In the midst of seeking revenge, no authority figure attempted to identify those who opposed Hitler from those who had supported him. In the eyes of the new government and many Czechs, it was time to punish all Sudeten-born persons. So Paka was forced to get on a train or a bus from Prague and travel to somewhere in Germany. She had never lived in Germany, but she was not given a choice. Neither my parents nor I ever found out what happened to her.

The person I loved and who loved me, my other mother whom I had seen every day for almost nine years, suddenly disappeared from my life. No more breakfasts with Paka, no more trips on the tram or seeing her happiness when she received a letter from her mother, which she'd sometimes let me open. Life was different without Paka—I missed her very much.

My childhood seemed to be full of disappearances of persons I loved: Grandmother Sophie, Uncle Richard, aunts and uncles and now Paka. As a young boy I did not understand what happened and was not aware of the causes of these disappearances: anti-Semitism, nationalism and racism. Yet I felt the pain and loss, and for a while I cried at night.

Chapter 7
My Jewish Grandparents:
Joseph and Sophie

Both Joseph and Sophie Marcus Stein disappeared from my life before my fifth birthday. Joseph had died in 1938, just before the Nazi occupation, when I was less than two years old. I have no memories of him. In black and white photos taken during the last few years of his life, I see a well-dressed older gentleman, slightly stooped, and assisted by his two adult sons, my father and Uncle Richard. He seems weak from the cancer he was battling yet surrounded by his supportive family. I do have a few sweet memories of Grandmother Sophie, who visited our home regularly and often brought food she had cooked for us. After the war I learned that she was arrested and sent to a camp at age 78.

Joseph and Sophie had four children—Richard, Karla, Kamila and Victor, my father. Joseph Stein was a successful grain merchant who sold hops, malt and barley to farmers and also to breweries in Bohemia-Moravia, Germany and Austria. His business was both wholesale and retail, including a store with both Catholic and Jewish employees.

The Stein family lived in the town of Kolín, about 35 miles east of Prague. The Jewish community was established there as early as the 14th century, and Kolín had the second largest Jewish population in Czechoslovakia. The Steins attended a local synagogue, where my grandfather was one of the leaders of the congregation. They lived a comfortable life in a large house and sometimes traveled to Germany or Austria for business or a vacation. After Joseph retired, he and Sophie moved to a comfortable apartment in Prague.

Then the German army invaded Czechoslovakia in March 1939 and changed everyone's lives. Although my family and relatives now officially lived in the Protectorate of Bohemia and Moravia, there was no protection for Jews, Catholic and Protestant clergy, socialists and communists, gays, Jehovah's Witnesses or anyone who opposed the Nazi occupation.

Hitler ordered Adolf Eichmann to establish the *Zentralstelle Für Juedische Auswanderung* (Central Office for Jewish Emigration) in Prague. Eichmann's goal was to expel all Jews from the Protectorate of Bohemia and Moravia. At first he encouraged Jewish families to leave the country, and more than 26,600 persons managed to emigrate. In my own extended family, a few relatives were able to reach England, Palestine or the United States. But once World War II started, fewer countries accepted immigrants, and all emigration stopped in October 1941. Jewish families were trapped in the Nazi web and most perished. Most Czech Jews were sent to Terezin and eventually to Auschwitz. The Nazis required that all Jewish men, women and children identify themselves and register with the authorities.

Jews were increasingly barred from most economic activities, and much of their property was confiscated. Businesses owned by Jews, such as my father's bentwood factory, were seized by the Germans, using threats and force. Overall, it is estimated that Germans stole half a billion dollars worth of Jewish property in the Protectorate of Bohemia and Moravia alone. (Dean 2008)

Everyday life was seriously affected by the occupation. Jewish families were denied items such as sugar, tobacco and clothing. Jewish schools were closed and, in August 1940, Jewish children—including cousins Gerti and Robert, who were sister and brother, and myself—were excluded from Czech public schools. My parents were able to enroll me in a private school located in downtown Prague.

Jews were allowed to ride only in the back of the second car on trams and were excluded from all but two hotels, Fiser and The Star. In Prague, Jews were required to sit in separate sections of restaurants and forbidden to use public swimming pools. In September, a dusk-to-dawn curfew was imposed on all Jewish households; radios were confiscated; Jews could withdraw no more than 1,500 Czech korunas (about $75) a week from their bank accounts. Jewish actors, musicians and technicians were not allowed to work in the film industry or in show business. Jewish doctors could practice only in the Jewish community; they could not take care of Christians. In April 1940 Jews were banned from public service and membership in all social, cultural and economic organizations and were even banned from popular areas of Prague such as the banks of the River Vltava.

The Nazis defined a Jew as a person, irrespective of his or her religious affiliation or self-identification, who had at least three Jewish grandparents who also were members of a Jewish congregation such as a synagogue. All Jews had to report to local police stations, where their identity papers were stamped with the letter J. In Prague, on September 1,1941, Nazis imposed a rule requiring Jewish men, women and children over the age of six to wear a yellow Star of David marked with the word *Jude* on their outer clothing. Later that month all remaining synagogues and Jewish places of worship were closed.

A person with two Jewish grandparents was classified as a *Mischling* of the first degree, while a person with only one Jewish grandparent was classified as a *Mischling* of the second degree. The term *Mischling* meant "mixed-blood," a legal term used in Nazi Germany to describe persons considered half-breeds or mongrels. Only those *Mischlinge* (plural) who were "privileged," meaning they were not raised as Jews and did not attend a synagogue, were exempt from this regulation. I remember my mother sewing yellow stars with the word *Jude* on all of my father's coats and jackets. Neither my mother nor I were required to wear yellow stars, because our official papers indicated that we were Catholics. I was exempt because I was not raised as a Jew before the occupation. (Bauer 2001); (Zapruder 2015)

During the occupation, most Jews were forced to move to smaller apartments, and in January 1941, families who lived in the better sections of Prague were forced to move so that Nazi officials and high-ranking Czechs who supported the Nazis could become the new occupants.

Grandmother Sophie Markus Stein was forced to give up the large apartment she had shared with her husband, Joseph, and move into an old tenement building in a poor district of Prague. She lived in the small apartment with her longtime maid, Anushka. As Sophie became frailer, she needed Anushka to give her insulin shots, help her dress, shop and cook and take her to medical appointments.

I have one vivid memory of Grandmother Sophie. I was probably five years old when she visited our apartment on the outskirts of Prague. She wore a dark gray coat with a small black ribbon commemorating the death of her husband. She carried a small casserole, which she placed carefully on the kitchen table. When she lifted the lid, there was an inviting aroma. I saw several pieces of chicken liver floating in clear chicken broth, one my father's favorite snacks. He loved to spread a little of the liver paste on a small piece of rye bread or a cracker.

Sophie gave me a taste of her delicacy on a cracker. It had an interesting flavor, memorable because I did not know whether I liked it or not. After a while she, my father and mother settled into our living room and closed the doors behind them. I stayed in the kitchen reading a book and had another taste of chicken liver. When Sophie returned to the kitchen, she was weeping. She gave me a big hug and whispered what would be her last words to me: "I love you."

Chapter 8
Reporting for Annihilation

I believe this was the last time my father saw his mother. The deportation of Jews to Terezin began on November 24, 1941, and Sophie was the first member of her family forced to leave. In looking back at what happened many decades ago, I wonder how she felt. Throughout her life she had been embedded in a large family. She had nine siblings. As a married woman she was the mother of four. But the Nazis did not allow any of her adult children to travel with her. Only persons assigned to the camp could travel on the train that day.

I continue to try to understand why my aging and ailing grandmother was forced to move from her comfortable apartment so that a Nazi officer could live there and steal many of her belongings. Why were she and tens of thousands of other people ordered to put their belongings into one suitcase, leave their homes and report to a dilapidated train station on the outskirts of Prague for deportation? Why was she separated from her adult children and friends who might have helped her survive? Why was my grandmother's diabetes medication taken from her when she arrived in the Nazi-run concentration camp? And why was she left to die a horrible death?

It was simply because she was Jewish. This murderous Nazi policy of killing all Jews from Nazi-occupied territory was made public by Reinhard Heydrich. Following Hitler's wishes, he ordered removal step by step by first clearing Jews out of Berlin, Vienna and Prague. More than 88,000 Jews lived in the Protectorate in the summer of 1941; by the end of the war the Nazis had sent 77,603 Jewish men, women, and children to Terezin. (Bryant 2007:47)

Once they arrived at the camp, the men, women and children were separated. Women, young and old, were marched to the women's barracks. Any medicines carried by the prisoners were confiscated, including Sophie's insulin, which she needed to survive. (Hajkova 2016)

She probably protested and tried to hold on to her medication, but she could not.

Sophie had to fend for herself without any medical help while living with hundreds of strangers in a huge old facility. She became very ill and died in 19 days. A few months later three of her four adult children were also deported in 1942. They all perished in concentration camps.

The forced evacuation of Czech Jews began in October and November of 1941 when about 6,000 men, women, and children were sent to the Lodz ghetto in Poland. Among those forced to leave their homes was my cousin's grandmother, Marie Perutz. Before she left Prague, her Czech doctor provided her with several morphine sulphate pills, which she could use if needed. She found life in the Lodz ghetto intolerable, and when she was told she was going to be sent to another camp, she swallowed the morphine and died there. She would probably have been sent to Auschwitz to die.

Most Czech Jews, including most of my relatives, were deported to Terezín, a ghetto/concentration camp north-west of Prague. It was located about 40 miles north of Prague. Although Terezin's main purpose was to assemble Jews from Czechoslovakia, Austria and Germany and ship them to the death camps in Poland—mostly Auschwitz—the Nazis presented it to the rest of the world as "a self-governing Jewish settlement." They wanted to construct the fiction that these Jews were given control of their community. H.G. Adler, a historian and survivor, called Terezin "the most gruesome ghost dance in the history of Hitler's persecution of the Jews." (Adler 2017)

While my parents' world was crumbling, I was starting first grade. My parents tried to protect me from their terrible reality, so I knew little of what was happening to my relatives.

Yet I saw the German occupiers every day, and I knew there was a war going on between Nazi Germany, the *špatní kluci* (the bad guys) and the Allies—England, the United States and Canada—the *dobří kluci* (the good guys).

Among adults there were many rumors about what was happening to Jewish families: the orders from Nazis, sorting and packing clothing and possessions, reporting to a central location, processing by Nazi guards, confiscation of all personal property, humiliation and degradation. Such was the lot of all Jewish families. Anxiety increased dramatically when orders started to be delivered to Jewish homes. These orders were usually delivered at night by messengers announcing when individuals or families were to report to a given location. The Jewish community provided young volunteers to help the sick, infirm and aged pack for the transport and to carry their luggage.

In Prague, Jewish men, women and children had to report to the exposition hall at the trade fairgrounds in the northern section of the city. It was surrounded by barbed wire. Wooden shacks with dirty walls and no indoor sanitary facilities housed the internees. The only latrines were a few filthy outdoor ones located some distance from the building. Each person or family was directed to a very small piece of bare ground in one of the shacks, called a "living space" by the Nazi guards. The dreaded SS controlled the processing of people.

At the fairgrounds, each adult was called up to a desk to complete forms that were in German and Czech. The guards checked names and bags, made bodily searches and confiscated all personal property such as watches, wedding rings, money and jewelry. Everything had to be turned in: keys to houses, apartments and cars, food and fuel ration cards, cash and valuables and personal documents. To make people less suspicious, the SS issued receipts for the items confiscated. The SS lied by telling everyone that all items would be returned once they reached their destination. In reality, the Nazis stole it all.

This humiliating and oppressive process could take several days and sometimes included harassment and beatings from the SS. Those who collapsed were sent to the Prague Jewish Hospital. If they died, the doctors were ordered by the SS to indicate that such death was due to a previous condition or illness.

Heda Margolius Kovály, who was deported around the same time as my grandmother, describes the chaos at this assembly scene:

"The inside of the exposition hall was like a medieval madhouse. Several people who were seriously ill and had been brought there on stretchers died on the spot. A Mrs. Tausig went completely crazy, tore her false teeth out of her mouth and threw them at our lord and master, *Obersturmbannführer* Fiedler (the German officer in charge). There were babies and small children who cried incessantly and, just beside my parents, a small fat bald man sat on his suitcase playing his violin as if none of the surrounding bedlam were any concern of his. He played Beethoven's Concerto in D Major, practicing the same passages over and over again." (Kovály 1986)

Once processed, people were marched from the fairgrounds to the Holesovice railroad station, escorted by SS guards and the Czech police. They were told what belongings they could take. Adults were limited to 50 pounds each while, children were limited to 30 pounds.

Kovály writes that during the early years of the German occupation, prisoners were marched to the railroad station during the day. As non-Jewish citizens of Prague watched the procession of Jews carrying their meager belongings, "the men took off their hats and many women wept." After a while the Nazis switched the boarding of transports to a time when the streets were empty, in the middle of the night or before dawn, under the cover of darkness. (MacDonald and Kaplan 1995)

In many Nazi-occupied countries such as Czechoslovakia, Poland, Belarus, Ukraine, Latvia, Lithuania, Estonia,

Holland and France, the local police were responsible for much of the day-to-day dirty work of controlling, ordering and harassing Jews. This freed many German soldiers for frontline fighting rather than policing the civilian population. (Dean 2008)

Between November 1941 and April 1945, about 141,000 people were sent to Terezin. Most Czech Jews were sent there first and then were shipped in closed cattle cars to Poland. About 95 percent of all the people who were "sent East" on these trains from Terezin to Auschwitz were murdered there. Yet people also died in Terezin. About 33,500 were killed there or died of disease, malnutrition, starvation or various medical conditions including, toward the end of the war, typhus.

Terezin itself was run by only 28 SS soldiers supported by 150 to 170 Slovaks and Czechs who served as guards for the ghetto/camp. Guards were rotated frequently to prevent contact between Jewish prisoners and Czech guards. (USHMM 2018)

At the railroad station in Prague, it was Czech policemen who forced other Czechs, Jews and non-Jews, into old passenger cars. Prisoners were pushed into cars as though they were cattle, a dehumanizing process that took several hours. The old passenger cars were jammed, and many people had to stand during the trip. The toilets were filthy and foul smelling from constant use. There was little heat during winter, and there was no food or water. Grandmother Sophie and several of my aunts and uncles were sent to Terezin in 1942 in such dilapidated passenger cars. Two years later my father may have been sent on the same railroad car. Grandmother boarded the train on a hot July day; my father boarded on a cold winter morning.

Years later he spoke about that day. "The weather was terrible, and the guards were worse. I wondered if this was the same car that carried my mother and siblings to Terezin. The ominous whistle blew and we were off to the unknown."

The last stop on the train from Prague was a station called Bohušovice where SS guards ordered all deportees to exit. There was more shouting, pushing, shoving and even beatings. Everyone was checked again by other SS guards, who confiscated any items they wanted. The deportees were then forced to march about two and a half miles to the concentration camp in the freezing cold, in snow, in rain, or in the heat of the summer.

Aunt Karla Stein and her husband, Rudolph Weigner, were shipped to Terezín in the fall of 1942, as were Aunt Kamila Stein, her husband, Richard Bergman, and their 30-year-old son, Erich. By the time Sophie's two adult daughters arrived in Terezín, their mother had died. Richard Stein, my dad's brother, was my favorite uncle. He and his wife, Elsa, often visited our home and usually brought gifts for me: stuffed toys, games, balls and, on one birthday, a Victrola and several long-playing albums. I liked listening to two Czech composers, Antonín Dvořák and Bedřich Smetana, with their lush sounds of violins and brass.

Richard and Elsa disappeared in 1942. They were also sent to Terezin and then put on another train to Maly Trostinec, a concentration camp in Belarus, where they were killed.

Around the same time, my mother's brother-in-law, Uncle Leo Perutz, was also arrested, sent to Terezin and later to Auschwitz, where he was killed. His Catholic wife, Olga (my aunt), and their children, Gerti and Robert, did not know what happened to him. When Robert, who was my age, asked about his father, he was told the same story I was being told.

"Your father is on a business trip; he'll come home as soon as he can."

We knew our fathers were missing, but we did not know where they were and what was happening to them.

All of my relatives were law-abiding citizens, well-educated professionals and responsible citizens, but the Nazis did not care. They were killed because they were born Jewish.

I learned after the war that when my father disappeared in the fall of 1944, he was sent to Terezín. As she had so many times before, my mother told me he was away on business. She also told me that he would come home as soon as he could. The second half of that turned out to be true.

Chapter 9
Father's Arrest

For part of the war, my father was a shadowy figure, in and out of my life. There were days, weeks and months when I did not see him. And then he appeared, almost magically, for a day or two and disappeared again. Whenever he came home I was overjoyed, but his comings and goings were a mystery. Years later I learned that the German occupiers forced Jewish men and women who were married to Christians to do manual labor. My father and my uncle Fred Prochaska, a Protestant married to my Jewish aunt Emma, had to work in road construction, even in a rock quarry, under harsh conditions.

I was seven years old in 1943 when my father came home for a day or two. On a clear and crisp Sunday, my parents decided to go from our home in the suburbs to downtown Prague. We all liked to walk, but that day the distance seemed long and my feet felt tired. I asked to take a street tram but my father said that the service on Sundays was slow and we would have to wait a long time. He tried to bribe me with the promise of ice cream, my favorite dessert, once we reached our destination. I grumbled but kept walking. In hindsight, my parents probably did not want to embarrass or upset me if my father was denied entry to the tram.

In August 1940, Nazis had restricted tram use: Jews were allowed to board only one designated tram carriage and were banned from single-carriage trams.

After a lot of walking, we finally reached the city's main square. Suddenly we were stopped by a Czech policeman who demanded to see my father's papers. I felt my throat tighten. My father said we were just taking a walk and asked what the problem was. The policeman raised his voice to tell my father that he was breaking the law by hiding his yellow Jewish star. My father protested that he was not hiding anything; he was merely carrying a briefcase in his left hand, which inadvertently blocked a corner of the yellow star my mother had sewn on his overcoat.

The policeman got angrier at my father and shouted, "Show me your identity card or I'll arrest you." My father complied quickly. The policeman spent a lot of time examining it, reading the front of the card, looking at his photo, sizing up my father and then studying the back of the card. My father's face turned redder and redder with anger. Mother tried to calm my father by taking his hand and whispering softly to him. After some time, the officer finally returned the identity card and warned my father not ever to hide his yellow star. We were all upset and retreated to the nearest café and sat down. The threat of arrest shocked all of us. With hands still shaking, my parents lit cigarettes. I tried to calm myself with a large ice cream cone.

The next morning my father was gone. I thought back to the prior evening. My parents often let me play in their bedroom before sending me to bed, but that night they sent me out. Mother took my hand and walked me back to my room and turned on the Victrola Uncle Richard had given me before he disappeared. She placed an album on the turntable, probably the "Cradle Song," a lullaby by Shubert. She tucked me in with a kiss and turned off the lights. "Good night, Peter. See you in the morning."

Of course I could not sleep; there was so much going on. I tried looking through the keyhole into their bedroom but couldn't see anything. I heard the opening and closing of drawers, and after a while I slowly opened the door. My mother was busy sewing a yellow star on the breast pocket of my father's sport jacket. He had to pay for each yellow star, which the Jewish community was responsible for distributing. Anyone caught without the badge was fined, arrested or even killed. Several other jackets with the star affixed lay on the bed. My father sat at a desk sorting papers. When he saw me, he came over, took my hand and walked me back to my room. "This second-grader needs his sleep. It's time for bed," he said gently but firmly. I did not want to disobey him. I felt tension in the air and had no idea what was happening. I was upset, and when I asked whether he was going on a trip my father answered, "Yes, but I'll be back soon." He rolled down the cover on my bed and gave me a kiss.

My mind was racing. Where was my father going? Was he in trouble because of the policeman who stopped us earlier today? Would he meet his brother, Richard? Would there be German soldiers where he was going? If, as he said, this was a short trip, why was he packing so much clothing, and why was my mother sewing all those stars on his clothing?

All the sewing and packing and sorting of papers masked the fact that the evening could easily have been the last time they would ever see each other. Maybe they dealt with their fear by staying busy.

My father did not know what to expect, because relatives arrested earlier were not allowed to write about their experiences. He had not heard from his siblings for more than two years, so he probably anticipated the worst. And he knew that his mother had died in Terezín two years earlier.

Early the next morning, my father reported to the trade fairgrounds where his mother and siblings had reported in the summer of 1942. He had the same abusive experience, nasty and screaming Nazi officers, abominable conditions and a dehumanizing process. My father had to list all his personal assets and turn in his watch, gold wedding band, wallet and keys. His bags and his personal clothing were searched for any hidden valuables. My father was angry but could not say or do anything in protest.

Years later he spoke about that day and about losing his mother and siblings at the hands of the Nazis. He understood the larger economic, political and social forces and the virulent anti-Semitism. But he could not forgive the brutal action of the soldiers, guards and executioners who killed so many Jews and his immediate family.

Chapter 10
Swimming in the Vltava

Some rooms of our third-floor apartment faced the river Vltava. I've seen photographs of my mother holding me as an infant and pointing in the direction of the river. My mother did a lot of swimming in that river and in lakes we'd visit during the summer.

My father also swam and taught me when I was quite young. I remember having fun in the water; we'd play games and splash a lot. But by my sixth birthday he was disappearing for stretches of time and could no longer swim with me. My mother was busy working in a factory and decided to get me a new swimming coach. One day we walked across the street and down the embankment to the local pool. I met my new coach, a tall young man, who was not smiling. He was all business and wanted to start right away. "I'll teach you the right strokes, but no fooling around," he said. "You're here to learn." But I did not want to learn swimming from a stranger; I wanted my dad.

The pool area extended out into the river. The entire pool was made of wood, long planks covering all the sides and the floor of the pool. The open spaces between the planks allowed the river's water to enter and exit the pool. The good news was that there was never any chlorine to hurt my eyes; the bad news was that the temperature of the pool was identical to that of the river. Some days my teeth chattered and my skin turned blue, but if the instructor said the lesson was on, I jumped in. In June, the water was still chilly. July and August were fine, but by September the water was cold again.

First the instructor made me stretch, arms up, sideways twists, bends and lunges. Then he stood next to me with a long wooden pole and a vest. The vest was thick and wide and made of canvas. It looked like it could be used to torture people. The coach put the vest around my chest and tightened the straps attached to the back. He then pulled a thick rope through an eye ring, made a knot and wound the other end of the rope around the pole. "Time to get in; let's see you swim."

I climbed down the ladder into the cold water. He rested the pole on a railing that was about five feet tall and ran the length of one side of the pool. One end of the pole was attached to the rope holding my vest and the other end of the pole was in the instructor's hands.

"I'll hold the pole while you swim," he said. "Don't worry, I won't let go."

I was glad to hear I wouldn't drown. "OK, start," he shouted. I wanted to show him how well I could swim, so I started with the breaststroke, the one stroke my dad had taught me. As I swam the instructor slid the pole along the top of the rail. If I started to drown, the teacher could fish me out without having to jump into the pool.

When I reached the other end of the pool, the instructor told me that I was doing all right but not breathing properly. "It's one, two, three, kick—again one, two, three, kick—and extend your arms more."

I soon learned the second function of the pole. Suddenly, the coach let go of the rope and I started to swallow water and was choking. It felt like I was going to drown. "You messed up a stroke," he yelled.

The only way I could prevent being dunked was to do the strokes perfectly. Once when the coach released the rope, I went straight down. I hit the bottom of the pool and scraped myself. At times I became confused about what he wanted me to do; he expected me to learn the strokes more quickly than I could. By the end of the half-hour lesson, I was glad to get out of the pool. The swimming lesson had become more torture than fun.

After a series of more successful lessons that summer, I was ready for a test outside the pool. To graduate, I had to swim from one side of the river to the middle, turn around and swim back to shore. Even though I did not like the pool dunking, I knew I would not drown there. Swimming in the river without the safety vest was different.

As the day of the swim test approached, my mind was busy. Would the waves bother me? How cold would the water be? Would I get tired? All of this raced around in my mind as I tossed and turned in bed the night before the big swim.

I was nervous that morning and ate little. The sun was shining by ten o'clock, when my mother and I walked toward the river. My mother kept saying I could do it. "Relax, and just do your best," was her advice.

Before I got into the water, the coach told me that I should keep swimming until he told me to stop. When he saw my scared face, he added, "I'll be in a rowboat near you; don't worry!"

At first I felt fine, doing the breaststroke smoothly, just the way I'd learned it. I kept repeating to myself, one, two, three, kick, one, two, three, kick. But as I moved farther from the shore, the waves started to rise and the water felt colder and colder. Just keep moving, I told myself. The waves started to hit my face, and every time I opened my mouth to breathe I swallowed some water. Even the rowboat was bobbing up and down as the instructor shouted, "Keep going, keep going!"

He was comfortable in the rowboat, while I struggled in the choppy water. After more swallowing of water, I reached the side of the rowboat and touched it.

"All right, you're half done. No resting. Head back to shore." I hoped the return would be less choppy, but I was getting colder and my teeth had started to chatter. The shore did not seem to get closer, but I did see my mother waving. My adrenaline kicked in and I had enough energy to reach the bank of the river and get out. Mother wrapped a towel around me and gave me a long hug, saying how proud she was. When the instructor came over and told me I passed, I felt relieved. When we got home my mother made a cup of hot chocolate, just for me. I wanted to tell my father about my success, but he was away on one of his business trips.

Chapter 11
Ice Skating on the Vltava

In Prague, the Vltava River was usually frozen solid by December. Ice covered the entire river for miles, from Braník, where we lived, all the way to the center of town, under the Charles Bridge. But the ice formed unevenly, smoother in some spots but mostly very bumpy. That was the challenge faced by our group of seven- and eight-year-old hockey players.

These hockey games took our minds off the war and German occupation. We felt a certain freedom out on the river, away from prying soldiers and the other constraints on our lives. Before and after our games we talked about how Czech hockey players were better than German ones.

As soon as the river froze, we started to look for smooth areas of ice where we could skate. We'd scout as far as we could, through the snow and unseen bumps. When we found a spot, we walked off the smoothest area and figured where to put the goals. Then we cleared off the snow as best we could. We had no shovels or brooms. We used our feet and hands and tried to smooth out the bumps. The two goals were marked with book bags and shoes, and we were ready. We laced up skates, put on gloves, grabbed our hockey sticks and threw out a puck.

On the weekends we had more players, enough for four or five guys on each side. We took turns playing goalie, the toughest position because the puck was made of hard black rubber and traveled fast, maybe 40-50 miles per hour. We were only kids, but we learned how to flick our wrists as we shot so that the puck flew off our sticks, sometimes out of control. The goalie tried to stop the puck with his gloved hands, but the chest, face and mouth were also used. We'd keep playing unless the goalie had the wind knocked out of him or started to bleed. Then we halted the action, stopped his bleeding and tried to figure what to do with his bloody handkerchief. We all agreed that it was never a good idea to have one's mother find a bloody handkerchief.

We usually kept playing until we couldn't see the puck any longer. Or until a parent showed up and told us it was time to go home. On some weekends after the morning game, we'd wind up at the hot dog cart by the side of the river.

One Saturday, as my mother and I sat down for lunch, there was a knock on the door. It was cousin Robert, carrying a pair of snow-covered skates and looking tired. My mother hugged him and asked what he was doing here. "The river is completely frozen, so I decided to skate from my house to yours," he said, puffing out his chest. To me, he seemed to be boasting.

A few minutes later, Robert said he was hungry and asked if he could have some lunch. It was just like Robert. I was usually less assertive. He was almost a year older than me, a better student, stronger. I felt inferior to him, a feeling I did not like.

When Grandfather Antonín quizzed us about what we had learned in school, Robert did better in math and science. When I ate at his house, he ate faster. Mother taught me to eat slowly; I think he had gotten a different lesson. When we played hide-and-seek outside, I had trouble finding him, but he usually found me. And once when I was hiding, he decided to toss small stones in my direction. When one pebble hit my face, the game stopped. My mother reprimanded him, but his mother countered that boys will be boys and I needed to be tougher. She accused my mother of being overprotective.

My mother turned red with embarrassment and anger, took my hand and off we went. This was one of several arguments I saw between the two sisters during the war. It seems they had had a lifetime of competition between them; my mother was older, was expected to do more chores around the house and be more responsible. She was also shy, more of a loner. Her younger sister was sociable, popular, self-confident and more self-centered. I heard that my mother was favored by their father, who had sent her to France to study for a year. Olga stayed behind in Prague, found a boyfriend and married two years before my mother did.

For days after Robert's surprise lunch visit, I wanted to skate to his house. I wanted to show that I could skate as well as he did. My mother opposed the idea but finally agreed, as long as I skated with a friend. On the weekend, Daniel, my hockey buddy, and I set out to skate all the way to Robert's house. We skated for a long time, but the

Charles Bridge, a landmark for us, was not getting any closer.

Two older boys came skating from the other direction. "Watch out," they warned us, "There's a lot of jagged ice up ahead." We were determined to keep going, but we finally hit an area that was impassable. The ice had formed into little frozen, bumpy hills and valleys that prevented us from skating any farther.

I wondered how Robert had skated all the way. Then it occurred to me that maybe Robert had not skated all the way to my house. Maybe he had walked on the street part of the way. I would never know for sure, but I realized at that moment that things aren't always what they seem, and what people say is not always true. I heard so many stories at that time—about the cruelty of the Germans, about which side was winning the war, about Jews being unsafe—I didn't know what to believe about anything.

Chapter 12
Food Rations

In addition to missing my father, I saw less and less of my mother when I was eight and nine years old, during the last years of the war, because she worked in a textile factory. When she was moved to the evening shift, she was gone by the time I came home from school. But I could always rely on Paka to pick me up from school or let me into our apartment if I came home alone.

During the German occupation, ration cards were issued for everything—for meat, fat, milk, sugar and other foods. Each time an item was bought, a card was punched. As the war dragged on, there was less food and fewer ration cards. During World War II the American government also issued ration books for meats, canned foods, sugar, eggs and coffee to civilians so that American soldiers could be fed. Such foods could not be bought without a ration book, and there were strict rules about how to use them.

On Sundays, when Paka went out, my mother and I had lunch together. Because there was a coal shortage, we ate in the kitchen, the warmest room in the apartment.

Eating in the kitchen was easier for my mother as well. She could just dish food from the stove. She was tired from working five nights a week. One day she dished out a combination of cooked carrots, turnips, Brussels sprouts (which I did not like) and a mound of mashed potatoes topped with mushroom gravy (which I liked).

Mother hardly ever scolded me, but she was angry that day. As we sat down, she explained that we would have no meat, only vegetables, because the butcher had no meat. He told her that the Germans were inspecting all of his sales receipts and limiting deliveries. There was not enough food for German soldiers and, according to German authorities, soldiers had to be fed before Czech citizens. Because my mother was a longtime customer, the butcher would sometimes sell meat to her even when he said he had none if she promised to bring in the meat-ration coupons.

But I was the reason we had no meat that day. After a hockey game on the frozen river, we boys had stopped at a street cart and purchased hot dogs. We had given in to their irresistible aroma. A large mustachioed man—bundled up and wearing gloves—greeted us. Each of us ordered a hot dog. In Czech, they are called *párky*. The vendor took off one glove and poked a long fork into an open vat of boiling water. He speared two big fat *párky*, placed them on a scale, weighed them and sliced each one in half. He then sliced four pieces from a large round loaf of rye bread, smeared each piece with yellow mustard and placed a piece of *párky* into each slice.

His face lit up with pride, like a sidewalk artist who has just finished a quick portrait. Then he asked for four meat coupons and 20 Czech korunas. That's when the problem started. Each of us had a five-koruna coin, but no one seemed to have coupons for meat. Jan kept searching the pockets of his trousers, while Tomáš was searching his jacket and Edvard admitted that his mother never gave him a ration card. I was taking everything out of my knapsack. The *párky* smelled great, but things looked bleak.

After a hectic search I finally found ours. My mother, anticipating my needs, put the card in my knapsack. But that card was for me, not for three other hungry boys. I knew it was a bad idea when I handed the street vendor my card, which he took, punched four times, returned to me and said thank you.

I told the boys they had to pay me back soon. But I felt uneasy. When I got home my mother asked about the hockey game and whether I'd had a snack. When I told her the *párky* story she crossed her arms and rolled her eyes. Whenever my mother rolled her eyes, I knew I was in trouble. She said she was upset with what I had done and reminded me of the food shortages. I tried to defend myself by saying the boys promised to pay me back, but my mother said the boys could not give me their meat cards and no butcher would take them.

Months after the *párky* feast, I was reduced to eating fresh bread and mustard without hot dogs. While I learned to like mustard sandwiches, even trying different mustards for variety, I always looked forward to the one place in Prague where we could get a good meal: my grandparents' home.

Chapter 13
My Catholic Grandparents:
Antonin and Zdenka

Grandfather Antonín, my mother's father, worked as property manager for a prominent mill and landowner. The mill was located in an agricultural area about an hour outside of Prague. Over the years, my grandparents became friendly with a few local farmers; this became important during the Nazi occupation. The old practice of exchanging goods or items without using money—a system of bartering—was forbidden by the German authorities. Any such illegal exchange was punishable by arrest, imprisonment and even execution. But people had to survive, so they did whatever it took to feed their families and cooperate with the neighbors. These exchanges had to be arranged carefully and quietly.

Looking back at those years, I realize that my grandparents broke several Nazi orders so they could prepare as tasty a meal for their family as possible. Sometimes they were able to get a chicken or loin of pork, eggs or butter and pay for them with jewelry or clothing or money, whatever it took. My grandparents were determined to provide a good meal for their daughters and hungry grandchildren at least once a week, on Sundays.

Our visits continued throughout the war and a few were memorable, including one in 1944 when I was almost eight years old. My mother and I had to take two different trams to get from our home to my grandparents' apartment, located on a quiet residential street in an upscale neighborhood of Prague. German soldiers were everywhere, including on the tram, but my grandparents' place made me feel very safe and stable. I really believed they would protect me if anything bad happened.

Their apartment covered one floor of a five-story apartment house. As we entered the building we heard loud classical music, and we knew right away it was coming from my grandfather's apartment. My mother frowned. She worried about the Nazis finding out that our family was listening to the BBC, the British station that rejected "official" Nazi news. We walked up to the third floor, where my grandfather, wearing a suit with a vest, greeted us at the door. He usually wore a suit when we visited.

He shook my hand firmly. "Hello, Peter, how are you?" He was reserved, not into hugging or showing his feelings, yet somehow that handshake reassured me. He was slim, with neatly combed, thinning gray hair and a well-trimmed mustache. Sometimes he smoked a long-stemmed pipe that gave off a sweet scent. Most of the time he seemed formal, and he rarely smiled or told jokes.

By contrast, my grandmother was smiling and gave me a full hug, saying she hoped I was hungry. She was short, a little chubby, and enjoyed feeding everyone. She wore her favorite blue apron. It was clean when we arrived and would be fully covered with sauces and chocolate icing by the time we left.

My mother's sister Olga and my cousins Gerti and Robert arrived soon after us. My father and theirs were "away on business." We entered the dining room, decorated with landscape paintings and several of my mother's still life oil paintings of flowers. She had painted those scenes when she was a single woman studying art, when life seemed full of possibilities, not fear. The dining room table was set with plates, bowls, glasses, silver cutlery and linen napkins, all resting on my favorite tablecloth full of red, white and blue dancers dressed in Czech national costumes. The sight of this idyll made me feel happy, hopeful.

On the side cupboard sat Grandmother's chocolate cake. My mother joked that her cake looked so tempting, we should start the meal with Grandma's dessert. As we sat down, my grandmother announced the menu, *svíčkova*, a favorite meal. She brought out a large platter loaded with thinly sliced roast pork surrounded by large dumplings, steaming red cabbage and a brown gravy boat. Grandmother performed surgery on the bread dumpling by wrapping a thin string around it, slicing it into even round pieces and placing a slice on everyone's plate. When I wondered why she didn't use a knife to cut the round dumpling, my mother said that the delicate dumpling would split into pieces if it were cut with a knife. Thoughts of the occupation, of Germans patrolling the streets and of food rationing all vanished as we enjoyed Grandma's delicious food.

After the main meal and before dessert, Grandfather, Robert and I went outside to get some exercise. For me it was mixed experience. I liked to run around but did not like having to compete with my cousin. Grandfather started by asking about school. The question I dreaded was, "What did you learn this week?" I was a good student but did not like being put on the spot. I answered that in math we studied addition and subtraction and we began division. I could answer the simpler addition questions but got stumped when Grandfather asked me to add four different numbers. Robert yelled out "fifty-four." He could add sums in his head, while I still had to write the numbers down before adding.

More questions followed, division and multiplication. Robert was ahead of me on all questions. Grandfather called him a mathematician. I felt stupid. And then I tried to reassure myself by recalling that Robert was smarter because he was a grade ahead of me. Czech grammar came next and Robert was better in that, too. But my time was coming. After the quizzes, we'd kick a soccer ball around and then it was time for a race. Grandfather walked down to the end of the block, turned around and shouted, "On your mark, get set, go!"

Off we went, legs kicking, arms pumping, heads bobbing, faster and faster, huff, huff, gasping for air, lunging for the finish line. I beat him by a step. Finally, I won at something!

It was time to go back upstairs for Grandma's special *pishinger tort*, a multilayered cake made of large thin sweet wafers separated by layers of smooth milk chocolate and topped with more chocolate. Grandma served the cake, while Grandfather sat in his easy chair, reading a news-paper.

It was nearly six o'clock in Prague and five o'clock in London: It was time for the BBC broadcast. The women stayed at the table while Grandfather, Robert and I moved into the study, where he turned on his brown Blaupunkt shortwave radio. "Turn down the volume, please," muttered my mother.

He spread a large map of Europe on his desk, using black checkers to show territory controlled by the Germans and red checkers to show territory liberated by the Allies. The BBC news broadcast started with London's Big Ben striking five times to indicate the hour. It was followed by the opening bars of Beethoven's Fifth Symphony, the distinctive "Ta-da-da-da, ta-da-da-da." The announcer's English accent and deep voice felt like plush velvet: "Good evening. It is seventeen hundred hours and this is the BBC news coming to you from London." After the "Bulletin of Main News" was completed, a new announcer came on and spoke in Czech. He reported on the progress of the fighting and gave some details. After the broadcast, Grandfather showed us the areas where there was heavy fighting, and the Eastern front where the Russians were pushing the Nazis back to Germany. There was a lot of heavy fighting everywhere.

Grandfather also told us that interspersed in the broadcast were secret messages for Czech resistance groups about supply drops, sabotage actions against the Germans, and other code words. Despite my mother's concern, the volume on Grandfather's radio was turned up because he was hard of hearing but also because the Germans jammed the broadcast, making it hard to hear. We heard more and more crackling followed by an annoying buzz. It was almost impossible to hear the announcer.

That's when my mother entered the room, upset with the noise. "If the Nazis hear this, we'll all be arrested," she warned. He told her not to worry, because their neighbors were also listening. With more and more static, Grandfather finally turned off the radio. Then he spoke about the bravery of Czech soldiers who had joined the British army, which was fighting against the Germans. He told me that my father's cousin, Dr. Zdeněk Steiner, was a medic with the British air force. I was so proud that a relative, a Stein, was helping to defeat the Germans.

After the broadcast Grandfather warned us not to tell anyone what we just heard. "Be careful, please be careful," was his message. Of course, that didn't stop me from telling my school friends the next day what I had heard on the radio. During this time, I must have experienced what psychologists call cognitive dissonance. Everything I heard from Grandfather and the BBC contradicted what I was told in school or heard on the German-controlled radio and saw in newsreels in the movie house. As to the question of which side was really winning, I decided that Grandfather told the truth, not the Germans.

I remember another powerful visit, in June of 1944, when Grandfather ushered everyone into his study, my mother, me, Aunt Olga and my two cousins. Uncharacteristically, my grandfather got very excited. A map of Europe was spread out, and he stacked his red and black checkers in one corner of the table. He told us that a week earlier he had heard a BBC broadcast reporting the landing of Allied forces on the beaches of Normandy. He placed black checkers on areas held by the German army. Leaning over the table, he placed red checkers on five beach areas: American troops had landed on Utah and Omaha Beaches, British troops had landed on Gold and Sword Beaches and Canadian troops had landed on Juno Beach.

Grandfather said that Omaha was the bloodiest landing. It was surrounded by steep cliffs and heavily defended German positions. Many American infantrymen were gunned down by German machine gunfire before the men finally made it across the beach to the foot of the bluffs, then up the bluffs. Robert and I were fascinated with the details of the battle and marveled at the bravery of the American soldiers.

He continued to talk about the June 6, 1944, landing when more than 150,000 Allied soldiers stormed the beaches. There were many casualties but finally, at the end of the day, Allied troops secured the beaches. Robert and I were swept up in excitement as Grandfather proudly reported the news. We started to imagine the defeat of the German army and having our fathers back.

It was a day with my grandfather I'll never forget. As we were leaving, he shook my hand again and told me to keep working hard in school and to listen to my teachers. Then he whispered into my ear: "Don't worry. Your father will be all right."

Chapter 14
Tinsel from the Sky

Jana was screaming. "It's silver. We'll be rich!" Pavel, her younger brother, jumped up and down. "Silver, we found silver!" he shouted. I rushed to the pile of shining metal, which looked like strands of tinsel from a Christmas tree. Each cluster of tinsel was tied together with a narrow metal string. Jana and Pavel lived in the same apartment house I did.

It was the fall of 1944. We three, along with other neighborhood kids, often played in the thickly forested hilly woods behind our house in Braník. It was full of pines, perfect for games of hide-and-seek and our favorite game, war. We collected a lot of pine cones for our forthcoming skirmishes. During our battles, some of us became American soldiers and would throw pinecones at the other, German, soldiers. That day, there were just three of us. I was in third grade, Jana was in second grade and her brother had just started first grade.

"Do you think the Americans dropped this for us?" I asked. "What is this shiny stuff?"

The tinsel was scattered on the trees and in an open area, and Pavel was so excited he was ready to scoop it up and hide it in one of our forts. "Don't touch it," Jana told her brother. Pavel usually listened to his older sister or he'd get a quick hit in the back of the head.

I told Jana and Pavel that my grandfather had informed me American and British planes dropped the tinsel to blind the German anti-aircraft gunners. Pavel wanted to know how he knew that, and I impulsively answered that he heard about it on BBC radio. As soon as I blurted it out, I realized my mistake. "No, somebody told him," I corrected myself. I hoped Pavel would stop asking questions, because this kid could tell his father, who could report it to the police. I had to be careful at all times; that's what my mother always reminded me.

We kids could not fight the Germans, but we wanted to do something to end the war. We talked about spreading the tinsel around to help the Americans or putting it on some targets. We never settled on a definite plan.

When I told my mother what we found, she rolled her eyes and warned me not to get involved. "Leave that metal alone and tell no one you found it. What if the Germans question you?"

But when I told Jana and Pavel what my mother said, they were not happy. Jana wanted us to collect the silver strands, take them to the local police and get a reward. She was convinced we'd become rich. "What reward?" I asked. She said that she heard that the Germans were giving rewards for found silver. Pavel got excited again, yelling that we'd be rich after all.

I kept saying that we should not help the Germans. I refused to believe there was a reward waiting for us. Jana said she was going to ask her father and went off in a huff. I was wishing that we had never found the tinsel.

Jana was quiet the next day. She said her father wanted to talk to me. I was scared of Mr. Honsa, our building's superintendent. He had a bad temper and sometimes yelled at his kids or his wife. He yelled at me when I almost broke the front gate by swinging on it. And his breath usually smelled of cigarettes and beer.

I took my time walking down the three flights of stairs to his ground-floor apartment. Once I got there, I waited for a while before knocking on his door. He opened the door but did not look angry, and he asked me to sit down. He agreed that the story about the reward was phony, and that the Germans would confiscate the packs of tinsel and then ask a lot of questions. He warned us not to have anything to do with the Germans.

I was relieved and promised Mr. Honsa to keep it secret. Then he came up with a plan. He would give me a big bag to collect all the aluminum. I was to bring it to him and he would take care of it. I left his apartment feeling confused. My mother told me not to do anything, but Mr. Honsa said to collect the stuff. What should I do? Should I tell my mother what Mr. Honsa said and get her upset, or keep it a secret and just collect the tinsel? And what if someone saw me? I remembered my father telling me to always listen to my mother and not to upset her. I wondered what he would do. I wished I could ask him.

I tossed and turned that night, thinking about the decision I had to make the next day. In the morning, I went downstairs to get Jana and Pavel. When I knocked on their door, Mr. Honsa answered. This time he had liquor on his breath. He handed me a sack for the tinsel and warned all three of us to make sure no one saw us. He'd like to help us but had an emergency repair in our building. He reminded me that as the oldest kid I was responsible for doing it right. Jana's mother pleaded with her husband to go with us but Mr. Honsa told her he was too busy.

We three kids took the steep, winding, wooden-log stairs up the hill. About halfway up, we took a sharp left turn and walked until we came to a clearing where we had found the tinsel earlier in the week. Now that clearing was empty, but we were sure we were in the right spot. Where was the tinsel? We looked everywhere, even in our secret hiding place, but found nothing.

Jana finally said what we all thought: Somebody else had found our treasure. She started to sob. "It's not fair. We found it first." Pavel started yelling, "It's not fair. It's not fair." I was disappointed, too, but I felt something else, something stronger I didn't mention. Relief.

Chapter 15
Confession

I did not look forward to going to church. Both the Catholic and the Jewish religions are founded on the unquestionable belief in a powerful, all-knowing God who has everyone's best interest in mind. That was the view of God I received from my Jewish father and Catholic mother and in the religion classes we were taught in the second and third grades in Prague.

But I had trouble reconciling these beliefs with what I saw in the world around me: German soldiers marching all over town, taking people's seats on the trams, stopping innocent people, making us scared all the time. What kind of God would allow that? And then there were the food shortages, bombings and the disappearances of relatives. My mind was full of questions. If there is a God, why were my father, my favorite uncle and other relatives missing? Why did the Germans make my father wear a yellow star on his clothing? And why were those nasty looking men in long leather coats, the Gestapo, all over Prague? I couldn't ask anyone about this.

A year later I had new questions. Why did God allow Prague to be bombed? Why did God allow innocent civilians to be hurt and killed, and homes, hospitals and other buildings to be destroyed? And why wasn't my father back? On the occasional Sunday when I went to church with my mother, we were told by the priest to pray. But I did not know to whom I was praying and whether my prayers would do any good. My mother prayed a lot. But had her husband returned? Was she less fearful for praying? She was still exhausted from working in a German factory. Was this an answer to her prayers? I became more and more skeptical about the existence of God.

My mother was raised a Catholic, and she encouraged my first communion. She believed going to confession would show that I was really a Catholic and thereby protected from the Nazis.

One afternoon as school let out, Paka was waiting for me. She told me to hurry because we were going to a church and we had to get there on time. She reminded me of what my mother told me: don't tell the priest your father is Jewish. After a brisk walk, we reached the church. It was an old structure with beautiful stained-glass windows, a high arched ceiling and paintings of religious scenes on the walls. The church was very cold. My hands were cold, my nose was cold and my feet were cold. The churches were not heated because no coal was available.

As we entered the church, Paka, herself a Catholic, nodded toward a structure made of dark brown wood with carved ornaments on the sides, near the front of the church. That's where I was to go. It was called a confessional, and it looked scary to this seven-year-old.

My throat tightened as I entered the confessional. It was dark inside, and I immediately tripped over a kneeler.

I knelt down, clasped my hands in prayer and looked straight ahead at the screen and the drawn curtain that separated me from the priest. It was too dark to see anyone inside the confessional. Although I was still cold, I started to sweat. A deep voice came out of the dark. "My son, why are you here today?"

I mumbled that this was my first confession and that I was getting ready for communion. The priest told me to tell him everything I'd done, especially anything bad. I had rehearsed these lines a lot, but now I was stumbling over my words. "Forgive me, Father, for I have sinned," I started to whisper. I reported that I had lied to my mother. The harsh voice wanted to know about the lie.

I told her I finished all my homework when I had not. And then I told him about the time I got a free ride on the street tram by not showing my pass to the conductor. The voice interrupted to say I should not tell lies, that I must do all my homework and always show my pass. But he wanted to hear more. I confessed to stealing an apple from a store near my school. What I did not tell the priest was that I was angry that my father was away.

I expected to be punished and wondered whether the priest would hit me. The voice told me to say the "Hail Mary, full of grace" three times, and never to do any of these things again. "God will be watching you." I promised to be good and agreed to come to confession more often.

As I walked out, a little weak-kneed, I knew I had not confessed everything. I did not tell the priest that I had cursed a photo of Adolf Hitler on a billboard several times. And I did not tell him that in bed at night, I prayed for the defeat of the German army. I believed the punishment would have been much worse for those sins. He never asked me about my father.

I had had to go to confession because my school class was scheduled for communion in a few weeks. We were all in the second grade and studying religion, which was a required subject. In fact, we were graded in religion just like the other subjects. Luckily, we had a nice religion teacher, a young woman who met with us twice a week during the last class of the day. She told us a lot of interesting stories from the New Testament about the baby Jesus, Mary and Joseph and the three wise men. The book was full of colorful drawings of chubby hovering angels and of a Jesus and his family who all looked European, and in particular, German. In this book, Jesus had blue eyes and blond hair. What I learned in class was that God was in charge and would protect all of us.

Prague was full of churches and statues of saints, including those on the Charles Bridge, which I often crossed. Yet to my young boy's mind, neither God nor the saints seemed to be protecting the Czech country or my family. And God was certainly not protecting my Jewish relatives. How confusing this all was.

We had several rehearsals, including one in the church itself, but now it was time for our first communion. Our teacher tried to calm us. "The priest of this church will lead the ceremony," she said. "Remember to kneel, cross yourselves as you approach the altar, and, boys, no fooling around, please. This is a very holy event!"

That Sunday morning, I remember my mother helping me put on a freshly ironed white shirt, trying a few times to secure a tie. "It's too bad your father isn't here, he could do this easily," she said. "We'll get your grandfather to help with the tie."

I don't remember much of that day, but I can still see the girls dressed in white, each carrying a flower. I do remember the meal we had at my grandparents' apartment after the First Communion service. Somehow grandmother found a pork roast with which to celebrate the day.

Chapter 16
Hiding

Knock! Knock! Knock!

My mother opened the door to our apartment one day in early May 1945. I was right beside her. It was Mr. Honsa, the super, wearing his usual painter's overalls. He was breathing hard and his face was red, but today there was no liquor on his breath. I hoped he wouldn't mention the tinsel incident to my mother.

He told us that he had heard that the Germans were setting up explosives to blow up the road in front of our house. He said, "There's a cellar up the side street where we can all hide." His voice was urgent. "Please get ready quickly."

"Explosives?" my mother gasped.

Mr. Honsa said he'd heard from the underground that Patton's Third Army had already liberated Pilsen, about 50 miles away, and was on its way to Prague. "The Germans will try to stop them with explosives." Mr. Honsa quickly turned away and ran up to the fourth floor.

My mother moved into action. "Peter, put on a sweater and put a toy in your knapsack, grab your pillow and hurry." I often moved slowly, but not now. I was too stunned to ask questions. I wondered what toy to take and grabbed my favorite Sioux warrior. I wondered how long we'd be in hiding, but there was no time to ask. My mother rushed around the apartment, stuffing a few things into a bag. She snapped it closed and asked if I had everything. I was scared but put on a brave face. We ran down three flights of stairs, pushed open the rickety metal front door and turned right onto the street.

The front of our house faced the main road between Pilsen and Prague. In the distance we saw piles of bricks and cobblestones blocking the road. There were patches of bare dirt from where the bricks had been moved. Closer to us, several men were digging a pile high enough to provide cover for the Czechs, who would later shoot at German soldiers. Suddenly, several men carrying rifles ran by us. Tricolors of red, white and blue, the Czech colors, were pinned to their coats. I thought I heard gunfire from the direction of downtown Prague.

Barricades were also set up near a truck depot close to our house where German troops had been stationed. Those intimidating soldiers were long gone. Now, toward the end of the war, the German soldiers were either old or very young, as Hitler pressed 15- and 16-year-olds into the war effort.

Despite my mother's bad leg from the bike accident years before, we picked up our pace. We moved through our neighborhood—past the ceramics store, past the beer garden, with its long tables now empty—and turned right up a small street that curved away from the main road. I knew that street well because my friends and I had played there, exploring backyards and playing cowboys and Indians.

After a short walk, we saw a small house with an open cellar door where we would hide. I peered into the dark basement and started to climb down a rickety ladder. A voice shouted from the basement, "Don't worry. The ladder will hold everyone." It was Mr. Honsa again, this time steadying the ladder. My mother followed slowly, favoring her leg. Several neighbors were there already, and so were Jana and Pavel. They had a deck of cards so we could play our favorite card game, war. The basement was damp and cold. A few light bulbs hung from the low ceiling. I saw a few chairs and a folding card table. There were no windows and it smelled musty.

It was getting darker outside as the cellar filled up. Mr. Honsa announced that the lights would be turned off soon because German soldiers were patrolling the streets. Those needing the bathroom should use the woods next to the house. He warned us that no one would be allowed to go out during the night.

Soon the lights went off, but the adults kept talking. I couldn't sleep, so I listened. One man was convinced that the Americans would liberate Prague. He heard that Gen. Patton's Third Army had already liberated part of our country and would soon be here from Pilsen. A second man disagreed. He said Roosevelt was too weak and that Stalin and the Russians would free us. Some argued that it would be Czech partisans who would take care of the Germans. One man shouted, "Our boys will take care of those Krauts."

Mr. Honsa chimed in by saying that he had heard the SS were fleeing the city but breaking into basements and shooting women, children and old people. That scared everyone, and the chatter stopped.

My mother spread out a blanket and used her warm winter coat to cover both of us. "Will the Germans find us?" I asked. She held me tight and whispered not to worry. "The Germans will be gone soon." I wondered whether our house would be destroyed by the Germans. She told me to close my eyes. The adults took turns watching the basement door. A few people snored, but I could not fall asleep. My mind was racing.

Suddenly I heard the sound of gunfire again—cak, cak, cak—followed by a loud explosion. Someone started to sob; an older man had trouble breathing. Mr. Honsa became excited, saying it was the Russian army chasing the Germans. Another man challenged him, saying that it could be the Germans chasing our brave boys. The shooting quieted down and then stopped as I finally fell asleep.

In a dream that night, my Catholic grandfather rescued us from the basement. He found us, told us the Czechs had won and brought us food. We were all happy.

My dream was interrupted by a soft knock on the metal door. I grabbed my mother. I wondered if the German soldiers were here. Would we be shot? Mr. Honsa, watching the door, whispered, "Quiet, quiet." We heard the knock again and then heard a Czech voice saying softly, "*Ahoj, ahoj* (Hello, hello). Honsa?" Slowly, Mr. Honsa climbed up the ladder, opened the door and helped a man down the ladder. I recognized him from the neighborhood. He wore a Czech army jacket and carried a rifle.

"Neighbors, our Czech boys, with help from the Russians, drove out the Germans. The war is over."

My mother threw her arms around me. Everyone laughed and shared hugs. Jana, Pavel and I danced around in a circle. The war truly was finally over.

Chapter 17
Father's Return

From May 5 to May 8, 1945, the Czech resistance fought the remaining German army in the streets of Prague. History remembers this as the Prague Uprising. German tanks fired into buildings, aiming at Czech fighters and citizens. There were many street battles, and buildings were pockmarked with bullets. Some buildings, including a church, were badly damaged. The wounded were left on the streets until they could be pulled to safety by brave Czechs. About 2,000 Czech fighters died during the fierce fighting, and about 10,000 were injured.

Most of the fighting happened in downtown Prague. Our neighborhood of Braník was relatively quiet. We would hear distant shots, probably from a tank or cannon. The usually busy main street was empty. There were a few pedestrians and bicyclists but almost no trams or cars. Shops were closed because they had no products to sell, and it was dangerous for shopkeepers and customers to be out. People made do with what little they had.

By May 9th things seemed to be quiet, and there were no sounds of downtown fighting. But where was my

98

father? Mother and I took turns scanning the main road in front of our apartment house. We watched a two-lane road connecting Prague with Pilsen. On the afternoon of May 9th, I was at my window perch watching the street when a Russian army truck suddenly pulled up in front of our house. I yelled to my mother and we ran down the stairs and out the front door. I ran across the street and stood facing the back of the truck, searching the faces. Two Russian soldiers helped men and women off the truck. Most looked weak, and some were almost like skeletons. It was hard for them to stand up to get off the back of the truck.

At first, I did not recognize anyone, but then I spotted my father, wearing the same gray jacket with the yellow star he had worn when he left "for a business trip." I screamed and jumped up and down, pulling my mother's arm. "*Tatinek* (Daddy)!" He jumped off the truck, holding a dirty sack in one hand. We cried with joy. He was thin but in good spirits. Before the war my father played soccer and tennis and skied; perhaps that fitness had helped him survive. He gave me a strong hug and pulled me to his chest. Suddenly I felt that my world was complete. We were a family again.

The Russian army truck roared away, spewing black diesel smoke into the air as we crossed the street back to our home. My father let me carry his sack. I was so glad to see and help him. My mother, who smiled for the first time in a long while, asked how he managed to get a ride from the Russian soldiers. He said the soldiers had looked for prisoners who had something to exchange for the trip.

He had a few silver coins hidden in the lining of his jacket, and he paid the soldiers for the ride so he could get home as quickly as possible. And he wanted to get away from the typhus epidemic spreading in Terezin toward the end of the war. He said the ride on the old army truck was long and bumpy, but he did not mind. He was free. That day I finally learned why my father disappeared: he had been a prisoner in a concentration camp.

Years later I learned that Terezin was both a concentration camp and a transit ghetto, mostly for Czech Jews. With the arrival of German and Austrian Jews, it also became a ghetto for the elderly. A majority of the 148,000 Jews transported to Terezin were sooner or later deported to the East and murdered in Auschwitz in Poland. More than 33,000 people died in Terezin of diseases stemming from malnutrition and towards the end of the war, typhus.

Men and women were separated and children were sent to "youth homes" elsewhere in the camp. Everyone between the ages of 16 and 60 was assigned to labor duty. (Hajkova 2014)

In 1964, my father and I visited Prague. I wanted to see Terezin while he did not want to go. I kept insisting. On a gray day in Prague, we boarded a bus for the two-hour trip to Terezin to pay our respect to relatives who had been imprisoned there. A rush of memories must have come back to my father as the bus approached the town. He spotted one building, a woodworking factory, where he reported daily as a prisoner.

We got off the bus and walked to a crematorium. I had not realized that Terezin was also a killing camp and that those who died were cremated in one of the four gas ovens. It was a gloomy looking building whose operation was launched in October 1942. My father's mother, Sophie Markus Stein, was cremated there and her remains were placed in a mass grave nearby. I recalled a grandmother who was kind and liked to cook chicken livers for her son.

From there we walked to a tower called the Small Fortress.

"That's where Aunt Mana and her 15-year-old daughter, Sonja, were imprisoned after they tried to escape," Dad said.

I had met Mana the previous evening in Prague and heard about her courageous attempt to flee.

When we saw the front wall of the camp, which still bore the German sign, *Arbeit Macht Frei* (Work Sets You Free), I saw anger in his face and then tears in his eyes.

"Peter, it was all a lie. Work did not save our lives. They killed us."

He spoke about his mother, who had had her insulin taken away and died here and his sisters and their husbands who were killed in Auschwitz. He cried for people he loved and missed terribly.

We walked to the barracks where he'd lived and tried to sleep every night with scores of other men. Now only part of that room remains as it had been. The triple-decked wooden beds were a stark reminder of Nazi cruelty. The men were forced to sleep on hard wooden platforms with little protection against the bitter winter cold. My father choked up as he recalled those times, and I started to cry, grateful that he found a way to survive, and devastated by the memories of those who had not.

Black and white photographs hung in the buildings that had once been dormitories. They showed half-dead men and women dragging through mud and snow in torn shoes or with rags around their feet. My father spoke of the bitter winter of 1944, when the men in the barracks huddled together just to keep warm. The little they ate consisted of stale bread, a watery soup with maybe a few pieces of potato or carrot at the bottom of a tall pot, and a dark chicory drink called coffee by the guards and something else by the prisoners. Most of the men and women suffered from intestinal disorders. Malnutrition was rampant. My father traded anything he found for something to eat, but there was little to be found. He was perpetually hungry, thirsty and cold, everyone's experience in Terezin, he said.

He did not know it on his wedding day, but my father was fortunate when he married a Catholic. Instead of being sent to Terezin shortly after the Nazi occupation, he had spent part of the war with other Jewish men doing forced manual labor in and around Prague. In 1944, when the Germans were losing the war, all Czech Jews like him who were still alive were arrested, rounded up and shipped off to Terezin.

My father said that his fluency in German helped him. Occasionally he overheard conversations between guards about deportations or police action in Terezin itself and managed to move out of harm's way. When the German guards spoke angrily about the way the war was going, he tried to make himself scarce.

In propaganda films and radio broadcasts, the Nazis presented Terezin as a "model camp for Jews." In 1944, the

Swedish Red Cross was invited to visit the camp to see, firsthand, how well the Jews were treated. My father told me how the Nazis reconstructed shops and decorated the town, renovating a recreation park and a concert hall. The bakery was suddenly stocked with fresh bread and pastries; the butcher's shop stocked sausages; the candy shop carried chocolates. Selected prisoners were dressed up and told to stand or sit at strategic spots along the specially designated route for Red Cross inspectors.

In the afternoon, the Germans staged a "friendly" soccer game between two teams of prisoners. In the evening, there was a spirited performance of the children's opera, *Brundibár,* in a community hall built especially for this occasion. The Swedish Red Cross inspectors believed the German propaganda and praised the quality of care in Terezin. After the Red Cross left, the movie props were disassembled, the food and goodies disappeared, and many singers, musicians, and actors affiliated with the propaganda film were sent to their deaths in Auschwitz, including most of the children who had sung in *Brundibár.* My father was terribly upset by the Nazis' ability to fool international inspectors. Life in Terezin became much worse after the visit as the Nazis reasserted their authority.

We boarded the bus back to Prague in silence. Other passengers who had been chatting on the way there were now quiet. Some held handkerchiefs, sniffling, trying to deal with the horror they had witnessed. Some spoke Czech. A few recalled relatives who had died there. Some spoke German, perhaps not understanding how their countrymen could commit such atrocities. Several Swedes must have been trying to understand how the Swedish Red Cross was so easily fooled.

When we reached Prague, my father took me to his favorite tavern, where we had several beers and continued to reminisce.

Life Remembered in Photographs, Prologue through Chapter 17

Prologue

Peter in his office in 1993, where he met students to discuss Holocaust denial.

Chapter 1: Disappearances

Mother and I about 1937 in our Prague apartment.

Dad and I in front of his Prague office.

Chapter Two: Meeting

Victor Stein and Zdenka Kvetonova, married in Prague's Old Town Hall, May 1934.

Uncle Leo Perutz, his wife Olga (my mother's sister), and cousins Gerti and Robert before the German occupatio.n

We lived in an apartment house in Braník, on the outskirts of Prague.

My father, Lt. Victor Stein of the Czechoslovak Army, prior to the German occupation.

Chapter Four: Occupied Prague

SS officer Reinhard Heydrich, (on right) known as the "Butcher of Prague," who implemented plan to murder all European Jews.

An SS officer like the one that Peter encountered on the tram to school.

Peter in the second grade of his Prague school, 1943.

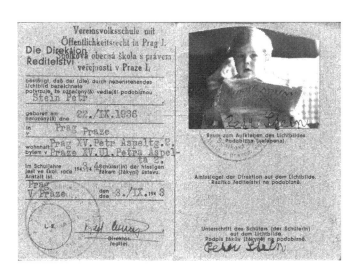

Peter's school transportation card, issued in German and Czech, 1943.

Father's work permit card with Nazi stamps, 1944.

Chapter 5: Allied Bombing of Prague

Forty B-17 planes of the 8th Air Force of the United States Army bombed Prague on February 14, 1945.

Chapter 6: My Other Mother, Paka

A happy toddler walking with Mom and Paka.

Going ice skating with Paka, 1943.

Chapter 7: My Jewish Grandparents

Joseph and Sophie with their children years before WWII.
Only two persons in the photo survived the Holocaust.

My Jewish grandparents before the German occupation.

Chapter 8: Annihilation

The euphemism "work will make you free" was displayed in many death camps, including Terezin, in this photo.

Jewish families arriving in the concentration camp of Terezin.

Richard Stein, my father's brother, liked to play and often brought gifts.

Chapter 9: My Father's Arrest

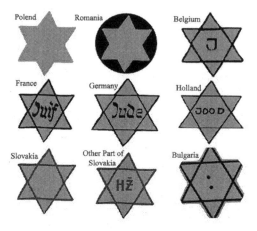

During the Holocaust Jews were forced to wear the yellow star. The star in the center, with the word "Jude" (Jew in German) was worn by my father.

Ink drawing by Leo Haas, a Terezin prisoner, shows the over-crowded conditions at the camp.

Chapter 10: My Catholic Grandparents

My Catholic grandparents, Antonin and Zdenka Kveton, provided loving support throughout the war.

Chapter 16: Hiding and Uprising

In May 1945 the Czech resistance fought German troops in Prague.

Fighting in the streets of Prague.

Chapter 17: Father's Return

Terezin liberated by Soviet troops; father returned on a Soviet Army truck.

Cattle cars that shipped thousands of Jewish families to their deaths returned the few survivors back to Terezin at the end of the war. Photo by Victor J. Stein.

Part II

Life After World War II

1945-1948

Chapter 18
The Post-War Years in Prague

The three years between my father's return from the concentration camp in 1945 and the time my mother and I left Prague are fuzzy in my memory. The Nazis were defeated and Czechoslovakia elected a new, democratic government. The people's hopes returned, but our small country was caught in the larger global struggle between Russian communism and Western democracy.

Between my ninth and 12th birthdays, I experienced more turmoil, a reflection of a lot of personal, family and political changes. The best thing was having my father back. We went swimming again, and he helped me master the breaststroke, which I still use today when I swim.

Sometimes we ran to a nearby field to kick a soccer ball back and forth, and he showed me some new moves. Some weekends my parents and I took walks around the city, often ending up at my favorite ice cream shop.

But I also felt sad after the war. I learned what had become of my Jewish grandmother Sophie, Uncle Leo Perutz and my father's siblings, all killed in the camps. I very much missed Uncle Richard, my father's older brother. Thinking back, I remember a warm sunny day when I was three or four years old. We had a family picnic in the park near our home. Richard brought a beach ball, which he inflated and started to kick around. He took off his jacket, loosened his tie and was ready for fun. We kicked and chased the ball across the playground.

In our apartment, Richard would sit on the floor of my room and we would invent games. He liked to have fun and he loved me. Thanks to him and his wife, I owned a small zoo of dogs, bears, giraffes and whales supervised by one friendly clown. As the war progressed and Richard disappeared, the friendly clown I had played with was displaced by fiercely battling toy soldiers.

The other person I missed terribly was Paka. She had been not only my second mother but like a good older sister. The feeling of abandonment I experienced the day she disappeared has stayed with me. Her quiet but confident way had been my anchor. Prague was lonely without her.

During the war, my life was circumscribed. I had some friends in school, but there were only a few kids living in our neighborhood. I usually went straight home after school. I did not have play dates, nor did I join any organized sport activity the way many American kids do. I often felt different from the other children. I was part Jewish and part Catholic, and my father was missing. I was shy and quiet and kept to myself. Sometimes I wandered to the football field in our neighborhood, but most of the boys were older and I could not keep up with them. I wanted to play, but I mostly watched from the sideline.

The German occupation ended in May 1945. Perhaps to get me out of Prague so they could have time for themselves, my parents sent me to a two-week sleep-away summer camp.

I don't remember how I got there. Maybe my father drove me, or perhaps they put me on a train with my cousin Gerti. I was ten and she, a responsible 13-year-old, was going to the girls' camp near mine. The camps were in an area called Krkonoše, a mountain range located in northern Czechoslovakia. One large hut housed the boys. Next to it was a large hut for girls.

This was to be my first camping experience, and I was not ready for it. At home, I had my own room and lots of privacy. Life at camp was just the opposite. Everything was done in public. The 20 or so boys in my group, ages 10 to 15, slept in one large room. Each of us shared a bunk bed with another boy.

The older boys made it clear they would sleep on the lower bunks, a privilege of age. Sleeping in a double-decker bed was a new experience for me. An older boy got into the lower bunk, and I had to climb over him and managed to step on him a few times. He was not pleased and did not bother to help me. When I reached the top bunk, I worried about falling off in the middle of the night.

Some of the older boys liked to pick on the younger ones. At home I could set my own pace, and if I needed help I would get it. I was on my own here and things moved much more quickly. In the morning the boys splashed a little water on their faces and hair and rushed to breakfast to grab a freshly baked roll and hot coffee. I was slow with washing, dressing and tying my shoes, so by the time I arrived at the breakfast area, most of the food was gone. I was also used to privacy in the WC and found it hard to get used to a group bathroom. The bathroom had no doors, and I was embarrassed to use the latrine with others around.

One day a couple of boys started to taunt me. "Look, Stein is finally sitting down on the throne," and "C'mon, Stein, we don't have all day. What's taking you so long?" They always used my family name, and after a while I felt they had anti-Jewish attitudes. They never called me a Jew, but they didn't have to. I understood what they meant.

Another time they mocked me: "Stein has white underwear, like a girl." That one hurt. Did girls really wear white underwear, or were these guys making it up? "You're a mama's boy," they taunted. I wanted to get back at them, but I had never learned to fight and the guys sensed that. One day I saw one of the guys who had picked on me wearing ripped and dirty underwear. I laughed quietly to myself.

But there were some things that got positive attention. I was a fast runner, especially in sprints, and the kids started to call me Jeep. I liked the nickname. It meant I was being accepted. And one day the counselors introduced a game called capture the flag, which also relied on speed. We formed two teams, and each team had a flag to protect while trying to capture the other team's flag; there were offense and defense in the same game. Each team chose a secret base to hide its flag. Players from one team could be tagged by players from the other team in the other team's territory and vice versa. Captured players then became members of the opposing team, giving that side a numerical advantage.

Players attacked their opponents with pine cones. These pine cone wars improved my mood because I knew how to throw and aim cones. I had played that game in Prague. The counselors appointed two older boys as captains, and they took turns choosing players according to their throwing abilities and speed. The first day I was one of the last boys chosen, but because I was a fast runner and pretty good at throwing, I was chosen earlier the next time.

For several days, we had vigorous flag wars, with lots of running, changing strategies and virtually no supervision. The counselors disappeared once we started, and the contest got rougher and rougher. The older boys started to throw the cones as hard as they could and plenty of bruises, bloody knees and scrapes resulted. I got a bloody mouth from a fast-moving cone and a bloody knee when I slipped on wet stones. The next day one kid got hit in the eye, and he was rushed to a clinic in town. That evening the director of the camp suspended flag wars for the rest of the week and told the counselors to supervise our activities. We were unhappy with the decision; we wanted to keep the battles going.

I also experienced positive change during my time in camp. I started to stand up for myself, and I felt less like a mama's boy. I learned to do more things for myself, such as dressing and organizing my area in the bunk. On the train home from camp, my cousin Gerti mentioned that I seemed to be more confident and that I seemed to feel better about myself. I felt proud when she said that.

Chapter 19
Catching Up with My Father

My father received a degree from a business college in Prague in 1921. In 1927, with help from a relative who was a successful businessman, he started and operated the Standard Bentwood Manufacturing factory on the outskirts of Prague. The bentwood manufacturing process involved wetting the dry wood by either soaking or steaming it, then bending the wood as it hardened into curved shapes and patterns like tennis and ping-pong rackets. I remember visiting the factory one day and seeing piles of twisted and burned wood. My father explained that heating and bending wood was risky because there was a limit to how far the wood could bend before it snapped. He said some wood would always be wasted, no matter how carefully it was produced.

Sometime between 1941 and 1942, the Standard factory was confiscated and run by the Nazis who started to manufacture other products made out of wood, such as rifle butts. When the war ended in 1945, my father tried to get his business back but ran into legal issues raised by the new government. In February 1948 the Communist Party seized the government and confiscated most private businesses, including my father's. He never got his factory back.

He was fortunate to be hired as the manager of a sports cooperative called Drusport. This organization produced and distributed various sporting goods, sport and military uniforms and recreational equipment. Drusport was owned and operated by its members, and they owned or rented a large warehouse in downtown Prague with a store in the front.

One Saturday morning my father took me to the store and encouraged me to explore the warehouse area. I discovered tons of interesting items: water canteens, large and small flashlights, axes and camping equipment. There were soccer, rugby and ice hockey jerseys. I found piles of military uniforms: American, British, French and Russian, for officers and enlisted men. Some uniforms hung from metal racks, while others were stacked in piles; some were brand new, others had dirt or smudges on them. Had each uniform been worn by a soldier in battle? I wished those uniforms could talk. There were no German uniforms: Father opposed having any in the store.

After rummaging around for a while, I found a beige-colored pith helmet. It was the kind worn by British soldiers when they fought Gen. Rommel's German troops from 1940 to 1943 across the North African desert. I imagined myself a British soldier fighting the Germans. I placed the helmet on my head and started to feel strong and brave. I wanted to have a weapon in my hand so I could attack them. When my father found me, he asked whether I was ready to fight the Germans. But the helmet was way too large for my head, and when I turned quickly it flew off. We both laughed and he gave me a hug. We rummaged through the other helmets and finally found an American one that fit just right. We took it home, and every kid in the neighborhood wanted to try it.

On some weekends we took short trips in my father's 10-year old Tatra convertible, a car made in Czechoslovakia before the war. The car had only two doors, and I had to climb over the front seat to reach the back. During the summer my father would roll back the roof, and I loved the feeling of sitting outdoors as the car moved along the road out of town.

Most of the time the car stayed parked in an unheated wooden garage near our apartment house. The garage held two cars: ours and one owned by a friendly neighbor who took care of our car. During the Nazi occupation my Jewish father was prohibited from driving or owning a car. I loved riding in the sporty Tatra, but starting the car became a challenge, especially on cold days. It had to be hand-cranked and, because steel hand cranks were expensive, my father kept the crank at home for safekeeping.

Turning the engine on involved distinct steps by the driver:
- Pull out the choke.
- Depress the accelerator pedal a few times to prime the engine.
- Pull up the hand brake.
- Put the gear in neutral.
- Switch on the ignition.
- Insert the hand crank into the small opening at the front of the car (the driveshaft of the engine).
- Turn the hand crank.

Before turning the hand crank on the front of the car, my father put on a pair of leather gloves for better grip. Once the engine started, he had to quickly remove the crank before it could fly off. Both he and the car were in danger of getting hit if it did.

On good days the engine would start after several turns of the crank. On bad days, he'd try a number of turns before the engine started. If the engine engaged slowly, it could flood with too much gasoline. If that happened he'd have to wait several minutes before trying again.

On one cold day my father planned to drive his Tatra to an out-of-town business meeting. As a treat, he offered to drop me off at school. But the streets were full of heavy wet snow, and when we reached the outdoor garage near our house we had trouble opening the gate. The lock was frozen. We shook and blew on the latch until it finally opened. Dad tried to crank up the car, but no matter how hard he tried, the engine would not turn over. He worked up a sweat and mumbled to himself. Just as he seemed ready to give up, the motor started and my dad jumped into the driver's seat, put his foot on the accelerator and gave the car enough gas to start. I was late for school but had a great story for my friends.

During the summer my parents took out-of-town driving trips. They loaded up the Tatra with a basket of food, a suitcase and gifts for relatives. My father did all the driving; my mother never learned to drive a car. We'd usually head for an area near the Vltava river where my mother's parents had a summer cottage. I'd hang out with cousins Robert and Gerti while my mother visited with her sister Olga. Olga's husband, Leo Perutz—Robert and

Gerti's father—was not with us. He was killed by the Nazis in Auschwitz, and we all missed him. But my cousins and I did not talk about relatives who died in the camps. We acted like kids and had fun running around in the woods and across fields full of haystacks.

At other times we visited my father's cousin Ema. She was one of the few relatives to survive the Holocaust. During these visits there was always a lot of kissing and hugging between the two families. My father and Ema grew up together, as close as brother and sister. They were prisoners in Terezin at the same time, and in the midst of chaos, cruelty and death they were able to support each other. My father said that knowing Ema was there kept him going. Their reminiscing gave me, then a 10-year-old, some understanding of what they went through and how very difficult it must have been to survive.

After lunch the adults lit cigarettes, usually a Czech brand that they said was not very good, but sometimes they shared French cigarettes, Gauloises. Those French cigarettes were made with dark tobacco from Turkey and Syria and had a strong and distinctive smell. Their conversation usually turned to remembering good times before the war and lamenting relatives who had died in the camps. The talk about death upset me, so I would go for a swim in the lake.

One dramatic incident on a cold Saturday in Prague gave me an understanding of my father's values. We were in the kitchen sharing a freshly baked roll with jam when we heard shouting from the street. We rushed to the window and saw a delivery man shouting at and hitting two horses which were trying to pull a wagon loaded with crates. There was a slight upgrade in the street in front of our house, and it was covered with snow. The horses had trouble getting traction on the icy pavement and kept slipping. The driver, becoming more and more agitated, whipped them. My father opened our window and yelled at the driver to stop. But the man ignored his screams and kept walloping the horses' backs and flanks. My father grabbed his overcoat and ran down the stairs. I watched the scene as he approached the man, waving his arms and shouting. They kept getting closer to one another as the driver shouted back. I really thought they would fight. Then the driver finally turned the wagon around and headed back down the street. He continued yelling over his shoulder. My father stood and watched the driver descend the road, then came back upstairs. He was upset but told me that cruelty to animals was not acceptable and that horses had feelings, like people do.

"Were you afraid?" I asked. I knew I would have been.

"No," he said. "The man had to be taught a lesson."

Chapter 20
A Daring Escape:
Jan and Tomáš Markus

After the war ended, my parents tried to normalize family life. Even as they were haunted by the loss of many loved ones, they tried to reconnect with relatives who had somehow survived the Holocaust.

I remember one of the reunions with cousins Jan and Tomáš Markus. Their father, Bedřich Markus was my father's uncle. Before I met them, I expected to see two old men, so I was surprised that both were young and energetic. They shook my hand vigorously and asked about my war experiences. I said I was glad that the war was over and the German soldiers finally left. Jan was older, looked stronger than Tomáš and seemed to be in charge. Both were intense. They sprinkled their scary stories with jokes, but their humor hid the tragedy of their parents' death and their own miraculous survival. Their story came out in spurts and then torrents. Sometimes they talked at the same time, even contradicting one another; their stories were amazing.

In the fall of 1942 the boys and their parents were sent to Terezin. About a week later their names appeared on a list of those to be "resettled to the East," to Ukraine. Based on rumors about the resettlements, they expected hard labor, but they felt they could do it: both boys were fit and healthy. Jan was 16 and Tomas looked older than his 12 years.

With thousands of other prisoners, they were packed into cattle cars. The boys said there was no room to sit and no food, and each wagon had only one bucket for water and one bucket for waste. These cattle wagons were fully enclosed and windowless. A number of people died during the trip from suffocation, illness or starvation. The trip lasted several days, and they had no idea whether they were going to a labor camp in the Ukraine or elsewhere.

When the train carrying the Markus family finally stopped, they immediately suspected it was not an agricultural labor camp in the Ukraine. In fact, they were in Auschwitz in Poland, hearing German soldiers screaming, "*Raus, raus*, get off the train! Quickly!" Everything sped up. Men and women were ordered into separate lines.

They became part of what the Nazis called "the selection process," a carefully planned event, during which many Jews would be sent straight to their deaths while some would remain alive temporarily. After the war, scholars learned that many of those who arrived in Auschwitz were murdered immediately. SS officers controlled everyone's fate. Those who looked fit to work were sent one way; the others were sent to the gas chamber. The officer in charge pointed to the left or the right. The elderly and women with children were forced on trucks and told they would first take showers, to "delouse."

The boys' father, Bedřich Markus, was 57 years old and their mother, Hana, was 42, both in good health and certainly not old. Maybe they looked old in the eyes of the SS doctor. The parents were separated from their sons and ordered to board a truck to the "showers." To make incoming prisoners less suspicious, the Nazis distributed soap and towels. They were ordered to undress and enter the showers for cleansing, but there would be no water. Once the doors were closed, pellets containing Zyklon B, a cyanide-based pesticide invented in Germany, were released through the showerheads, and all were gassed and killed. Bedřich and Hana Markus were murdered within a few hours after arriving.

Jan and Tomáš were ordered to stand in a different line and assigned to do manual work. First they were sent to a separate building for registration and tattooed with a number. Their hair was shaved off. They were disinfected and forced through real showers, which they said were very cold. Once deloused, prisoners were issued striped pajamas, a cap and a pair of wooden clogs. Then they were marched to the housing blocks, already overcrowded with other prisoners. They had no idea of what had happened to their parents. For months they searched the camp but never found them.

For more than two years, the boys were forced to do hard manual labor. Most of those working prisoners died of malnutrition and various diseases. Miraculously, through determination, stamina, a strong will to live and sometimes luck, Jan and Tomáš survived Auschwitz. By the fall and winter of 1944, as the German army was losing the war, Allied armies were closing in on Nazi concentration camps. The Soviet army was coming from the east and the British, French and Americans from the west.

The Nazis wanted to hide evidence of the brutal conditions in the death camps, so they began to move prisoners to Germany. There were no trains or trucks available, so prisoners were forced to walk. These were called death marches, and the largest was from Auschwitz in the winter of 1944-45, one of the coldest winters on record throughout Europe. Russian troops were already liberating parts of Poland but nine days before the Russians arrived in Auschwitz, nearly 60,000 prisoners were forced to march out of the camp. Jan and Tomáš marched for days and nights in the bitter cold with very little food, water or rest. About one in four prisoners died on the way, more than 15,000 persons. When the Russians entered Auschwitz on January 27, 1945, they found only a few remaining prisoners.

Jan and Tomáš were forced to march through snow to the city of Wodzisław, about 35 miles from Auschwitz, in the western part of Upper Silesia. The boys said that SS guards harassed or shot anyone who fell behind or could not continue. After several harrowing days, Jan and Tomáš were loaded onto a very old unheated railroad car. They did not know where the train was going, but there were plenty of rumors, mostly that they would all be killed once the train arrived in Germany. (USHMM 2018)

In the chaos of the fighting, military trains were given precedence over trains carrying prisoners, so the train the boys were on often slowed down, stopped, started and stopped again. During the slow ride, Jan and Tomáš started to whisper about a possible escape. The older boy wanted to try it, but the younger one felt it was too dangerous, fearing the German guards would shoot them. But they kept their eyes and ears open for any opportunities. The boys tried to look through the boarded windows as often as possible. One night the train stopped completely.

Jan, ever alert, heard voices outside—not in the usual German or Polish but his native language, Czech. He signaled Tomáš and they both listened as the guards standing outside the train chatted about a local beer pub. They realized they were probably not far from their home village of Řevnice.

Jan tried opening the door to the passenger car and, to his surprise, found that it was not locked. He insisted they escape, stressing they would be killed anyway when they reached Germany. "It's our only chance to survive; we've got to do it!" he said firmly. Jan took the lead. "When I count to three we're going to jump, OK?" Tomáš was still too scared to move. Jan pulled the door open and stood on the stairs of the car. "Do you want to die? Just jump!" Jan ordered. He counted again—one, two, three— and this time Tomáš jumped, followed by Jan. They hit the ground and started to roll down a hill.

The slope leveled off onto a gravel road parallel to the railroad track. Jan and Tomáš sprang to their feet without looking back. They feared being shot, but no one fired or yelled at them. They jumped over a low fence and ran across a barren field, hoping to find shelter and food. They were starving, thirsty and exhausted. They had not had a decent meal in two years. In Auschwitz they had been fed something the German guards called "soup," a terrible brown liquid with a little fat floating on top and, if one was lucky, a few vegetables sitting at the bottom of a large pot. The portions had gotten smaller and smaller as the Germans were losing the war. For most prisoners, eating the soup led to diarrhea, but there was nothing else to eat.

It was a bitter February morning as Jan and Tomáš looked for familiar landmarks. They hoped to find someone in or near the village who could provide shelter. Maybe someone who remembered their parents would let them in. They decided to look for the house of Mr. Promysl, who took care of their parents' garden before the war. They found the house and knocked on the door. Mr. Promysl opened the door, stared at the two boys and quickly pulled them in. He warned them not to walk around in their prison rags. "If you're seen, you'll be shot," he told them.

The noise woke up Mrs. Promysl, who scurried down the stairs. She was shocked to see how skinny the boys were and pushed them into the kitchen for food. She told her husband to get clothes for them and he quickly returned with pants, shirts, jackets, gloves and an old hat for each. He told the boys to eat quickly and leave. "If anyone sees you, we'll all be arrested. Feeding Jews is punishable by death." It was the boys' first real food in a long time, and they ate it quickly. There was no time to enjoy the freshly baked bread. The wife told them to leave their striped pajamas behind. She'd get rid of them.

The boys were on the run again. The sky was still gray, but the sun was slowly rising. They decided to look for their uncle, Dr. Alfred Markus, and his family, and after a determined search they found the Markus home. Anna Markus, Alfred's Christian wife, and their 18-year-old daughter, Vera, were shocked when they saw the starving boys on the doorstep. Because they spent many summers with Jan and Tomáš, Anna and Vera were close to the boys. Despite great danger to themselves, the brave women decided to hide the boys as long as they could. Dr. Markus, who was Jewish, had escaped the Nazis by fleeing to Shanghai, where he spent the war and was still away when the boys tried to hide.

However, the Markus home was not safe, because the Gestapo inspected the house regularly. After a few days, Jan and Tomáš gained enough strength for a hike to the Czech mountains to find another Czech family whom they hoped would hide them in greater safety. The boys could not risk taking a train and decided to walk. Along the way they hid in abandoned summer cottages.

They located an older couple who had known the boys' parents before the war. The couple agreed to hide Tomáš until the end of the war. It was too dangerous to have both boys there, so Jan sought a different hiding place with Anna Markus' brother, who lived in Moravia, another Nazi-occupied area. Both boys survived until the end of the war, when Jan and Tomáš reunited. Both grieved the death of their parents.

My parents and I were moved by the boys' amazing story of survival. After the meal at my parents' home, Tomáš and I played with my collection of tin soldiers. He knew a lot about uniforms and the different ranks in the Czech, British and, of course, German armies. One of the

German soldiers reminded him of a guard who harassed him in the concentration camp. He almost threw the tin soldier against the wall but stopped at the last minute. Tomáš and Jan became my heroes.

Chapter 21
Fighting Nazis in Russia:
Kurt and Malvinka Fanta

On another Sunday afternoon our apartment doorbell rang and I rushed to greet the guests. It was my father's cousin Kurt Fanta, holding hands with Malvinka, his new bride. Kurt wore a Czech army uniform with captain's bars and several shiny medals. He took off his officer's cap, revealing dark hair combed back straight, the way most Czech men wore their hair. He looked strong, with broad shoulders, but I noticed a mild limp. He introduced us to Malvinka, who also wore captain's bars on her nurse's uniform. Her round face had a friendly smile, and she wore her blond hair in a bun.

Kurt was my father's first cousin. His mother, Fina, was my father's aunt. Fina and her husband had moved to Palestine before the war, when they saw the persecution of Jews begin.

My parents led our guests into the living room, where the adults started to chat. It was a warm afternoon, and my father asked me to go downstairs to the Braník Beer Garden and get some beer. My father handed me our glass pitcher and told me to be careful with it. Instead of running down the stairs the way I usually did, I walked carefully, protecting the pitcher. When I reached the street, I made a right turn and in a few minutes entered the pub. Flowers and planter boxes alongside the wooden banquet tables created the pub's beer garden.

It was only a few minutes after noon and the pub was already active. A few families waited to be served the day's special, *Svitckova na smetane* (beef sirloin in cream sauce) served with a slice of *knedliky* (a bread dumpling) that soaked up the cream sauce. The smell made me hungry. In one corner, a group of Czech men ordered their first pitcher of beer for the day. During the German occupation, most of the patrons were German officers and a few enlisted men, while most Czechs stayed away from the local beer garden. It was nice to see the Czechs return.

The man behind the bar wore a white shirt, vest and a bow tie. His outfit spoke of an era well before the German occupation. He motioned to me and I politely wished him "*Dobrý den*" (good day), and then asked for beer, "*Pivo prosim*." The bartender knew who I was, because my parents and I had eaten in the garden several times after the war ended. He placed the pitcher under a beer tap labeled *Braník Svetly*. The barman turned the wooden-handled faucet as he tilted the pitcher on its side, creating a 45-degree angle. The golden beer began to flow, and he set the pitcher down to settle the foam. After a few minutes, he again filled up the pitcher so that the head rose above its rim. He picked up his skimmer and ran the straight edge of the steel tool over the surface of the glass to clear the froth. He pushed the pitcher toward me, and as I picked it up, he cautioned me to be careful, echoing the advice my father had given me earlier.

The walk back was a challenge. The sidewalk was bumpy. There were three steps down into the courtyard of the apartment building and three flights up a narrow winding staircase. I had a few breathless moments but kept my balance and did not spill a drop. I arrived in our apartment feeling very proud of myself. I'd have a story to share with my school friends on Monday.

The adults spoke about the good old days and wept for relatives who died in the camps. I listened with fascination to Kurt's stories about the war and about Czech history. After the Czechoslovak Army surrendered to the German army in the spring of 1939, some Czech soldiers fled the country to safety in England, France or the Soviet Union, all countries friendly to the Czech people. Kurt was a socialist, and he decided to flee to the Soviet Union. There he joined the First Czechoslovak Independent Brigade, which would become a unit within the Soviet army. The brigade of about 3,400 Czech soldiers played a key role in several battles, and its troops were some of the first to reach Kiev, the Ukrainian capital city. Kurt became an officer in this brigade.

Back in our dining room my mother served a typical Czech meal that she had prepared: roast pork with bread dumplings and sauerkraut. Our guests enjoyed it and asked for second helpings. I sat next to Kurt and waited for a chance to ask about his medals.

He spoke about the Czech soldiers who fought alongside the Soviet army and about the fierce fighting which continued day and night, some in bitter cold. He joked that it was the same frost that hit Napoleon and the French army in 1812 and, just like the French, the Germans had not expected it. German trucks bogged down in the snow and mud, and relief supplies for the troops could not get through. He said the Germans ran out of food and ammunition and the Russians, with help from the Czechs, captured almost 100,000 men of the mighty Wehrmacht's 6th Army. He said the Czechs fought hard and received medals for bravery issued by the Soviet army.

Kurt saw that I wanted to touch the medals, so he took one off his jacket. He said the Russians called it the "medal for courage" for fighting the German army. It was a circular silver medal with the Russian words *ЗА ОТВАГУ* (for courage) and a T-35 tank on the front. On the back were three flying aircraft. I was really impressed; I had never held an army medal before. I was amazed to have another hero in my family. My father had also been in the Czech army, but he had no medals or riveting stories of fighting.

Later my mother asked Kurt how he and his wife met, and he spun out the story. He was wounded during heavy shelling by the Germans and transported to a hospital away from the front lines. There he met Malvinka, one of the nurses on duty. They were separated when Kurt healed and returned to the front, but they found each other again as the war ended.

I asked Malvinka about her experiences during the war. She also escaped from the easternmost part of Czechoslovakia, called Ruthenia, to the Soviet Union. She spoke about nursing many soldiers and pretended to wrap a wound and place a bandage on my forehead. Then she reached into her pocketbook and took out several aspirins and pretended to swallow them. I loved her pantomime. She was definitely fun.

Then came a big surprise for all of us. Kurt said that Malvinka was also Jewish; there had been a small Jewish community in Ruthenia before the war. She had learned about the killings of Jews by Hitler, and when she finished nursing school she wanted to do her part in defeating the Nazis. She joined the nursing corps of the Soviet army. Kurt hugged Malvinka and announced that he was so lucky to have met her because she saved his life. I saw that they kept holding hands. I rarely saw such affection between my own parents.

Both spoke about the harsh conditions in the rural areas of Russia. At some point their Czech army unit, which was attached to a Soviet unit, was stationed near a huge collective farm in the western part of the Soviet Union. Collective farms were formed from many confiscated smaller farms so that the land and food production came under the government's supervision and control. Private property was severely curtailed.

On this collective, everything was scarce. For example, there was no indoor plumbing, only outhouses, and only one large bathhouse for the hundreds of people living and working there. Saturday was bath day for the girls and women, Sunday for the boys and men. I did not ask whether they changed the water between Saturday and Sunday. Kurt said that it was better to bathe early in the day; by Sunday afternoon the water was really brown.

I could not believe that everybody washed in the same water. Kurt told me that the people had no choice. Then he discussed the severe food shortages the Russians faced throughout the German invasion. The German troops slaughtered stock and poultry as they advanced into Russia, leaving little meat for the local population. Kurt said that they had potatoes, potatoes and more potatoes, with a few vegetables and a stray chicken. When they were lucky they had some bread. Malvinka kept nodding in agreement.

I saw this brave couple only a few more times. About a year later they moved to the new state of Israel to join Kurt's mother and her husband, who had escaped Hitler. They settled down in Haifa and opened a travel agency.

Chapter 22
Surviving Auschwitz:
Mana and Sonja Arendt

As my parents reconnected with relatives who survived the Holocaust, I started to realize that we were part
of a much larger family. Surviving relatives had amazing
stories of bravery. One was Marie Arendt, whom my
parents called Mana.

In anticipation of her visit, my mother spent hours
cooking, and the sweet smell of chicken and mushrooms
filled the apartment. As the hour arrived my father paced
near the front door waiting for her. He had not seen his
cousin since the last week of the war, when both were
prisoners in Terezin.

When Mana arrived, my father was so excited he tried
to lift her off the ground. She resisted, saying he'd hurt
himself, but my father was obviously overjoyed. They had
grown up together; now they were both in their early 40s.
Mana was also a good friend of my mother and asked how
she had managed during the occupation.

Mana kept hugging and touching each of us. I got a
big bear hug, and she kept repeating how grown up I

looked since she last saw me. She may have been thin and tired, but I remember her quick smile and the way she linked arms with my parents as we all moved into our dining room. Everyone's joy was obvious. It was one of the happiest evenings I can remember.

Over dinner, the adults spoke about the few relatives who survived and the many who perished. Mana, her husband and their 13-year-old daughter, Sonja, were among the first Jewish families to be deported to Terezin in 1942 and were then sent to Auschwitz. Her husband died in the camp. I learned that of the 87,000 persons deported from Terezin to Auschwitz, only about 3,000 returned at the end of the war. Mana and Sonja were among those few. As she spoke, I wondered how they survived.

Mana recalled the two terrible years she and her teenaged daughter spent in Auschwitz. They had very little food, and they were always hungry. One day some Polish girls who were prisoners told her that at around six every evening a little food was tossed out. They said that the cooks threw scraps—potato peels, the tops of carrots and stale bread—into large barrels sitting outside the kitchen. Later in the evening the bins were collected.

Mana said that to get anything to eat you had to act quickly, so she went to the back of the kitchen the next day as it started to get dark. She rummaged through the garbage for a few minutes, when suddenly a German cook came out the door to smoke a cigarette and spotted her. "You dirty Jew, get out of here," the cook yelled, and started to hit Mana with a wooden spoon, threatening to report her. Mana, summoning her best German, begged her to stop, saying she had a daughter who was starving and that the scraps were being thrown away. The cook spat on her, turned around and went back into the kitchen as Mana clutched the scraps and hurried back to the barracks to feed Sonja.

My mother asked whether Mana was afraid of what might happen if seen by German guards. I was shocked by Mana's answer. "We didn't care, we were so hungry. We thought about food all the time. The hunger made us half-mad." Despite the horrors she described, Mana's voice was soft. I thought about how brave she was, and I wondered if living through this hell made her stronger inside.

Mother said the women had gone through a terrible time. She put her arms around Mana, who was weeping. My mother kept saying, "It's a miracle you survived, it's a miracle." My mother also realized that the stories were going to get even more disturbing for her 10-year-old son, so she hustled me to bed. I did not want to leave and tried to listen from my room, but I could not hear much. As I dozed off, I tried to understand why the German cook was so cruel to poor Mana.

The next day Mana talked with my parents about the last year of war, and at last I heard the stories Mother had tried to protect me from. In late 1944 and the early months of 1945, Allied soldiers were defeating the German army, and the Soviet army was approaching Auschwitz. Mana and her daughter experienced the same death march that Jan and Tomáš Marcus had endured.

Mana and Sonja were forced to march for days with no food or water before being herded into a train headed from Poland to Germany. All of this was chaotic, and at one point the two women somehow escaped from the lightly guarded transport train. But unlike the Markus brothers, Mana and Sonja were captured by Czech soldiers serving the Nazis and were imprisoned in the cellar of Terezin's Small Fortress, a cruel location. They were weak from the march and then punished for their attempted escape by not getting any food. They survived only because some prisoners, including my father, brought them scraps of food whenever possible. The scraps were passed through one narrow window when the guards were taking a break.

As my father spoke of those days, he was near tears. He said that Mana and Sonja were very valiant, and they were skin and bones when they arrived in Terezin. I don't know how my father discovered that Mana was in the Small Fortress; perhaps someone told him about the new prisoners. I remember Mana crying and reaching for my father's hand. "Vicky, you were an angel to find food for us." My father said it was sheer luck and explained that a Czech fellow, a one-time soccer teammate before the war, worked in the Terezin kitchen and sometimes sneaked food out; my father was able to bring that food to Mana and Sonja.

The conversation turned to Mana's husband. She paused and sighed and spoke about the chaos in Auschwitz when they got off the train from Terezin. The German soldiers were screaming orders: "Men to the right and women to the left." She tried to hang onto Karl, but they were separated when a guard pushed her husband away. It was the last time they saw each other.

Chapter 23
Living in Limbo

It was a Saturday morning in 1946 and a chance to spend time with my dad. "Grab your soccer ball and I'll show you some tricks," he said. We ran down the stairs and to the playground. Before the war my father had been a very good soccer player and had played in an organized league in Prague.

He knew I was a fast runner but wanted to know if I could change directions while dribbling a ball. He sprinted down the field, then suddenly turned to his right and to his left. During the twists and turns he kept control of the ball. "Start slowly, keep the ball close. Now faster, around me, fake right and go left." It took a while, but I was getting the hang of it. We ran around, up and down the pitch until we were both tired.

Back at the apartment we drank cold water, and my father rolled out a new idea. He asked how I'd like to live in the United States. I was excited and scared all at once. I thought of missing my friends and having to make new ones in a strange place. I asked whether my grandparents would be coming with us, but my father said they did not want to move. I felt sad, knowing I'd miss them. Would I ever see them again?

I had many questions. When would we leave? Where would we go? And would all three of us go together? He assured me we would, but later I overheard that my father would stay behind; he still hoped to get his bentwood factory back so he could sell it. Any money from such a sale would help cover our future expenses in America.

Of course I was happy that the war was over and my dad was home. The German soldiers were gone; there were no air raids, no shootings, and everyone seemed more relaxed. On Saturdays, my friends and I would go the movies downtown and watch American films such as *Courage of Lassie, King Kong* and *The Great Dictator*. My favorite actors were the comedian Charlie Chaplin, tough guy Humphrey Bogart, the beautiful Elizabeth Taylor and the mysterious Ingrid Bergman. The films had Czech subtitles typed on the bottom of each frame. I loved the way these films started, with a growling lion introducing MGM films and a bare-chested strong man hitting a large gong at the beginning of every J. Arthur Rank film. The feature film was preceded by documentary films in black and white about animals in the wild: tigers, leopards, rhinos, gorillas. Films with sharks and octopuses gave me nightmares.

Whether to stay or leave Prague was the major discussion in our family. At one point my father said he would like us to stay, but he worried that life in Prague would get much worse. He believed the Communist Party would take over and everything would change. But a couple of times he said we were moving for my sake, so that I'd have a better life in America. That made me feel awkward. At one point I said, "Let's not leave, let's stay and we'll survive." But that angered my father. "Peter, you have no idea how bad our lives will be under communism; we have to leave." He tried to reassure me that Aunt Mary Anne and Uncle Leo Altheim, who had moved to the United States after the war, would take care of us. He told me that Uncle Leo, whom I had not met, was a nice man and a lot of fun.

A few weeks later my father pulled some books out of his old leather briefcase. One was about life in the United States, another was a book of photographs of New York City and a third was about American Indians. I started to look at the one about Indians and learned about the variety of peoples and cultures. There were about 500 different Native American tribes, and the book was full of photographs and paintings of warriors riding horses, families living in tepees, wearing clothing which was exotic to me, working on the land and fighting white settlers for their ancestral homes. The more I read, the more I liked them. The Indians looked noble and brave, and I could see they fought for a just cause. They became my new heroes.

I knew something about Indians because Uncle Richard, before he disappeared during the war, had given me a few small ceramic figures of Indian braves. The Indians usually carried bows and arrows, hatchets and knives. In comparison, on the rug where I played, my toy German soldiers were in action poses: shooting rifles and submachine guns, throwing hand grenades, extending bayoneted rifles, shooting a cannon, manning a rocket launcher or driving a tank. In the battles I staged, the

Germans used tricks to trap the opposition by sending out a couple of soldiers to lure the Indians into a trap. But the Indians caught on and usually defeated the German soldiers. The Indians were clever and outsmarted the enemy by hiding in one area of the folded rug, where the Germans would not find them.

The idea of a move really took hold a few months later, when Aunt Mary Anne Altheim came from New York City to visit us. She and my father were first cousins; their mothers were sisters. I was taught to call my parents' cousins by the respectful titles of aunt and uncle. She had escaped from Austria in 1938 during the *Anschluss*, the German annexation of her country. Because she had been an experienced stamp dealer in Vienna, she was hired by Macy's stamp department in the flagship Manhattan store.

My mother said that Mary Anne was always so well dressed that she could have been a fashion model. When Mary Anne visited us in Prague, she brought many gifts, clothes, food and, my personal favorite, Wrigley's spearmint chewing gum. My mother tried to persuade me to chew the gum only on special occasions, because it was not available in Prague. Mary Anne also gave me a small replica of the Statue of Liberty. She told me that the statue stands at the entrance of New York Harbor. The actual statue was a gift from the people of France to the people of the United States. I was impressed with the model and placed it on a windowsill in my room facing the nearby river. I imagined that I would see the real thing one day.

Aunt Mary Anne had many stories about the United States. When I could not follow her English, she spoke in German. She told me about the opportunities in America, and she was so persuasive that I could see myself in the streets of New York having a good time. She said that Uncle Leo and she would be our sponsors and that we could live in their neighborhood. But nothing could happen until we received American visas.

In 1946, when I was 10 years old, my parents applied for visas. Each of us needed a separate one, so three became the magic number. They thought the process would take a few months, but it took almost two years. The long wait was full of uncertainty. Would we qualify for visas? Would all of us get them at the same time? When would we find out? Several times we thought we were getting them, but they didn't appear. I lived in suspense. When would we leave? Would I stay in my current school for another year? How much time did I have with my friends?

I was confused about what I really wanted to happen. On some days I hoped to stay in Prague, on other days I was ready to leave immediately. When there were problems getting the visas, I worried about my schoolwork, especially passing the mandatory exams. And then I worried whether the authorities would let me leave Prague if I failed the school tests. Though I liked reading books about life in America, cowboys and Indians, the Wild West and Manhattan, I was not sure I would be accepted. Would I fit in?

I spent time worrying about a lot of things. For the fifth grade, I had been sent to a new school farther from my house. It was much larger, with high ceilings, wide hallways and heavy wooden doors. My old school felt warm and welcoming; the new one felt cold and distant.

None of my friends went to this new school, and most of the kids were older and bigger. The teachers were stricter and more formal, and schoolwork was more difficult, with a lot of homework and many tests. Instead of learning German, in which I had done well, we had to learn Russian, which I found difficult. My parents could not help me; they did not speak Russian, a strange language with a Cyrillic alphabet.

The old school was fun, with friends and nice teachers. We played a lot of active games—soccer, foot races and dodge ball. Now I had compulsory gymnastics. The gym teacher told us that in the spring of 1948 we would all participate in the first post-war *Sokol Slet*, a gymnastic event that celebrated Czech national pride. It was an honor to participate. Thousands of boys and girls would wear red, white and blue uniforms, the Czech national colors. We were told to practice hard so that we would represent our school well in floor exercises, the vault, a rope climb and rings. I did well enough in the floor exercises, in climbing the rope and the rings. But for some reason getting on the pommel horse was a tough challenge. I just could not jump over the vault, and when I tried I usually landed awkwardly and often slipped off the horse with a loud bang. I became scared of that exercise. A few boys laughed at me, and I felt ashamed of not being able to mount the vault. I preferred soccer or ice hockey played on flat surfaces.

As the big *Sokol Slet* event got closer, we had more and more practices, even on Saturdays. I did not like such regimentation. It was not fun. I came to dislike this huge gymnastic event.

Yet some school days were better. One morning our teacher marched our class down to the main lobby, which was decorated in red, white and blue, also the colors of America (I now knew). An American woman was standing next to a large table full of vegetables and fruits. We were all surprised to see an American; there were very few in Prague in those days. I recognized the strawberries, blueberries, apples and pears but could not identify a few brown crescent-shaped objects.

Our teacher asked whether anyone knew what these were. Edvard, who seemed to know everything, piped up. "They are bananas, and they grow in warm climates and turn brown as they ripen." The American woman suggested, in broken Czech, that we try the bananas. She took a knife, cut the bananas into small pieces and handed one to each of us. She showed us how to take the skin off. The piece I got felt soft and mushy in my hand, yet the taste was so sweet I licked my fingers.

Our teacher explained that these fruits and vegetables were brought to us by the United States as part of UNRRA, the United Nations Relief and Rehabilitation Administration, which was set up all over Eastern Europe to help countries rebuild. It was good to taste American fruit; living there might not be so bad.

But in February of 1948 there was another big political change. The Czech Communist Party staged a coup and seized political power. No one was allowed to publicly criticize Stalin and the communists. My parents warned me not to talk about politics in school, on the tram or with friends. It reminded me of the Nazi occupation. Now the teachers and our textbooks hailed the Russian liberation of our country from the Nazis and painted a rosy picture of life in the Soviet Union under socialism and communism. They started to criticize the United States and Western democracies. Photos of Joseph Stalin, the communist leader, now hung in classrooms, where previously pictures of Hitler hung during the war. The Soviet flag replaced the Nazi flag.

I had more immediate concerns. I did not do well in Russian or in botany class. The Russian language was difficult, and in botany there were tons of leaves and plants whose Latin names we had to memorize. There was no Paka to help me with schoolwork, and my parents were too busy. My mother helped sometimes, but she was organizing our move and my father was working long hours, trying to raise money for our trip. My parents hired a university student, who came to our house weekly to help me with Russian homework and keep an eye on me before they got home.

Sometimes I daydreamed about skipping classes, but I was too afraid of getting caught. While lying in bed one night, I realized that my school torture would end once we left Prague. And then I reasoned, since I was leaving anyway, why bother going to school? One morning I got off the tram at my usual stop in downtown Prague and walked in a direction away from the school. Head down and cap almost covering my face, I passed a lot of people. I was scared I would be recognized, so I made a quick left turn onto a side street away from the main square. The street curved left and right and opened into a small square with street vendors setting up their fruit, vegetable, baked goods and meat stands. I kept walking toward the river until I found a bench. I sat down and tried to sort my fears. Will anyone see me? Will they tell my parents? What will I tell my teachers tomorrow?

But I kept telling myself that since I'd be leaving Prague soon, they couldn't do much to me. This cheered me up. When my stomach started to rumble, I knew it was close to lunchtime. I couldn't go back to school, but where could I eat? If I went to the sandwich shop near the school, I might be seen. The historic Café Slavia had great open-faced sandwiches, but that was too risky. Since I had some money in my pocket, I decided to get a *párky* from a vendor on a street corner. With the war over, I no longer needed a meat ration coupon and could treat myself. I sat on a bench facing the river and enjoyed my hot dog with tangy mustard.

It was too early to go home. What to do? I had another idea. I was standing on the corner of Smetanova and Narodní streets. One street faced the river, the other headed to the center of town, away from the river. The National Theatre stood on one corner. I heard music and crept in through a partially open side door. I was familiar with the building because I had been there for a concert with my mother. I walked up a back staircase to the first balcony and sat down. On the stage was a tall man who was costumed as Neptune, god of the ocean. Dancing around him were water nymphs living in streams, lakes and springs. It looked like a lot of fun until another nymph came out of the pond crying. She was upset and Neptune tried to comfort her. They were singing throughout all the action, when suddenly they stopped. Everyone on stage turned to listen to a man from the pit who shouted directions for the singers. A few minutes later the music resumed. I could not see the musicians seated in the pit, but I heard their lush music. So this is what a dress rehearsal for an opera looked like.

I enjoyed the dances, the singing and the music so much that I lost track of time. When I checked my wrist-watch, it was four in the afternoon, and I realized I had to catch my tram home. On the way out, I asked someone the name of the opera. It was *Rusalka* by the Czech composer Antonín Dvǒrak, and it was opening the following night. I wanted to go to the opening but knew I couldn't. I could only hope my mother had no idea how I had spent my day.

Chapter 24
Getting an American Visa

Why did my parents want to leave Prague, the place where they had lived most of their lives? This is a question faced by many immigrants: Why leave a place you know well and go to a new country with a language you don't know and whose customs you don't understand?

As Czechoslovakia was becoming less and less democratic, life in the United States seemed more and more appealing. One dramatic event convinced my parents to leave. Father came home early one afternoon in February 1948 and seemed upset. He paced back and forth in the living room before finally sitting down next to me. He said that the day was tragic because the Communist Party had staged a coup, ending our democracy. Radio broadcasts were shut down, and the police sealed off streets downtown. He told me that the country was now under communist control with Soviet backing.

I told him that I too was surprised, because my school closed early and we were told to go home immediately. "Why isn't the Czech army protecting us from the communists?" I asked. My Dad said that Czech soldiers were confined to their barracks and ordered not to get involved. The police were in charge, but they were controlled by the Communist Party and therefore supported the coup. Some Czech generals also supported the coup, so no one would protect us. "Democracy is dead," he declared angrily.

I got another shock. He showed me the front page of the day's paper, *Národní Listy*, with many columns of white space where news stories were deleted. Even some of the stories that had been printed showed sections that had been deleted. I looked at the headlines:

The New Czech Republic under Communist Control!

Victorious February!

President Beneš resigns!

Stalin congratulates Gottwald, a Communist and new Czech leader!

I felt confused and afraid. "This is terrible; what can we do?" I asked. My father reassured me we'd be all right and would get the necessary permit to leave. A few months later, the political takeover directly hit our family. I was not told, but my father was being investigated by the new government, which under new rules had the power to confiscate all privately owned companies with more than 20 employees. Even though he did not get his bentwood business back after the war, he was investigated and harassed. During the investigation, he was ordered not to leave the country, and his passport was confiscated by the government.

Most of my parents' discussions of what to do took place behind closed doors. One evening my dad came into my room, sat on my bed and held my hand. He said my mother and I would go the United States soon, and he'd try to sell some real estate property he owned and join us later.

He spoke about how Aunt Mary Anne and Uncle Leo would help us adjust to life in America and that our lives would be better. He said there was no hope in a communist country, that life would only become more oppressive. I heard his words, was glad for his hugs, but did not want to lose my father again.

He kept reminding me to listen to my mother and be a good son. He said something I did not want to hear: the decision to leave was made by my parents for my benefit. I did not want such an obligation. I wanted to remain a kid and not have any adult responsibilities. But staying in Prague was not an option.

Getting an American visa turned out to be a long and complicated process. Both of my parents had to visit the U.S. Embassy, located in another section of Prague, several times. The first time, I went to the embassy with my mother. A Czech guard handed us a number. When the guard looked at me, I wondered what he thought. Did he envy me, or did he think I was a traitor for wanting to leave my country?

We waited a long time before my mother got to speak to an embassy official. The clerk, sitting behind a desk, handed her a form that spelled out the process of applying and the formal requirements. It was printed in Czech and English. She was asked to show a number of documents, including birthplace and date of birth, every residence since birth, educational records, tax records, proof of no criminal activity and photos. All of the documents had to be originals, no copies allowed. The application form itself looked quite long. She needed a certified money order to cover the application fee and the visa.

Over the next few months, my mother became busy collecting the many documents needed. She had to search for papers that were not available and, due to the chaos of the war, not easy to get. I assumed getting photos would be the easiest part. But when I showed the clerk my official tram card issued by the city of Prague, his face spelled trouble. He looked at my photo card and, with a stern face, handed me a one-page document titled "Photo Requirements":

- Photo must be printed on photo quality paper
- Size of photo must be 2x2 inches (51x51 mm)
- Size of headshot must be between 1 inch and 1 3/8 inches (between 25 and 35mm) from the bottom of the chin to the top of the head
- Must be taken within the last 6 months with a plain white or off-white background
- Must be a full-face view directly into the camera
- Must have a neutral facial expression
- Must show both eyes
- Must be wearing clothing normally worn on a daily basis

I immediately saw the problem. My face was turned to one side. There was a poster behind me. My face was not neutral; I was smiling. My head was too small and the photo was taken a year earlier. We had to search for a photographer. The few studios we found seemed very busy, and my mother insisted on a Saturday appointment so I would not miss school. The photographer she located was reluctant to follow the rules, but eventually both of our photos satisfied the stringent requirements of the U.S. State Department.

I noticed my mother was smoking more, perhaps to deal with the stress. Once, after a very long wait, my mother said this experience reminded her of a famous book by Franz Kafka who wrote about faceless bureaucrats requiring more and more documents. I agreed.

Getting a visa was also slowed by an old American law. It was the Johnson-Reed Act, passed by Congress in 1924, and it limited the number of immigrants who could be admitted based on the number of people from a specific country living in the U.S. in 1890. At that time the number of Czechs living in the U.S. was small, so the Czechoslovak quota was small. The law was designed to restrict immigration by Southern and Eastern Europeans, many of whom were Jewish. In fact, the Office of the Historian in the U.S. Department of State stated that the purpose of the Johnson-Reed Act was "to preserve the ideal of American homogeneity." Unfortunately, my parents and I fit into the category of less desirable Europeans.

Finally, one afternoon in the spring of 1948, I was greeted by my beaming mother when I came home from school. I spotted two plates on the kitchen table, each holding my favorite dessert, a chocolate éclair. My mother said it was time to celebrate. She reached into her pocketbook and pulled out two Czech passports and two American visas. "We've been invited to come to America. It's official."

I had not seen her so happy for a long time. I opened the visa and saw my photo. In the background were an eagle, the colors red, white and blue and the Lincoln Memorial. I felt proud that America had accepted us. Then I realized that she had only two visas. I wondered what had happened to my father's. There were more discussions: Should we all wait for him, or should my mother and I go first and he follow? My father said that before he could go, he needed to settle his finances so that we would have money to use in the States. What I didn't know was that he had no passport and couldn't travel anyway.

My parents seemed to have new energy. Suddenly visitors appeared in our apartment to try out my mother's piano, to sit on the red leather sofa (my favorite place to sit and spread out), to inspect the furniture and even to look at my bed. I didn't know what was happening; it all seemed strange. And I had decisions to make. My parents told me that I had to limit the number of things I could take.

Mother helped with my clothing, but toys and books were my responsibility. She suggested I spread out all my toys in one area of the bedroom and then make two piles: keep and give away. This was hard; the keep pile was much bigger than the giveaway pile. I didn't want to let go of toys, especially my collection of soldiers that helped me fight the Second World War. I could not give up my brave Apache Indians, and how could I give away my British and American soldiers? And what should I do with my large collection of German soldiers? I spent weeks trying to figure it out.

Maybe it was the paperwork, or those trips to the embassy, or the stress of the move itself that led to quarrels

between my parents. There were more and more arguments about what to take and what to give away, what to pack and how to pack, how to send things. As they became more nervous, they started to fight about whether the move itself was a good idea. My mother would have to leave her aging parents and her sister behind; my father had lost most of his relatives during the Holocaust, but he had friends, work colleagues and property.

And time was moving along, because our American visas expired after six months, so we could not delay. Father wanted to postpone getting a visa until he could sell his property, but the laws for the selling of commercial and private property were changing, becoming stricter. The Communist Party imposed severe limits on all commercial sales. They also imposed strict limits on how much Czech money could be taken out of the country.

Getting a visa was only preliminary permission to travel to America. The final admission to the United States occurred at the port of entry. There, an immigration officer decided whether to allow entry and the length of stay. My mother and I had visas, but we had no guarantee that America would accept us. What if we arrived and America told us "no"? And my father didn't know when, or if, he'd get out of Prague.

We all had to deal with a lot of uncertainty.

Chapter 25
Out of Prague

It was another cold and gray morning in October 1948 in Prague, an early sign of forthcoming winter. But this day seemed especially bleak as my parents and I left our apartment in Braník and walked down the stairs to a waiting taxi. My mother and I each carried a suitcase. My father had his old brown leather briefcase with him. The army-green knapsack I usually carried to school was on my back. The sky opened up and the rain poured down.

Inside the cab the only sounds I heard were the noisy windshield wipers. No one spoke; each of us was alone with our thoughts. Perhaps my mother was thinking about the parents she was leaving behind and wondering whether she'd see them again. Under the communist regime it would be very difficult, if not impossible, for her to return to Prague. Perhaps my father was wondering when he'd see his wife and son again. He was facing difficult decisions about getting funds out of communist Czechoslovakia to the United States.

It was hard for me to believe that I was really leaving my house and town. Through the taxi window I saw so many familiar sights: the field where we played soccer, the swimming pool on the river, a favorite ice cream shop, the movie house where I watched American films, and, after a sharp right turn, the central railroad station. I was trying to look brave, fighting back tears and biting my lip. "Don't worry," my father said. "Everything will be all right."

The taxi pulled up in front of a gigantic train station. The tall arched roof, with many straight and curved metal beams, was home to scores of pigeons nesting under its dome. Its vastness and darkness scared me. I half expected someone in a dark trench coat to come out of its shadows and grab me. The station was full of busy travelers, with many trains arriving and leaving. We looked for the manually operated bulletin board that announced train schedules and platforms.

A porter helped us with the suitcases, and we headed for platform No. 4, the train to Amsterdam. Each car of the train was marked and numbered. We boarded one of the second-class carriages; my mother said first class was too expensive. The porter carried our bags aboard and placed them in a reserved compartment. My mother, father and I occupied three of the four seats in the compartment. Mother placed a bag of food on the fourth seat. The upholstered seats were comfortable and covered with plush velour. Each compartment had a window that could be pulled down.

Despite my fear and tightening throat, I had to inspect the train. I counted 10 cars that would be pulled by a shiny black coal-fired engine. This was the longest train I had ever seen, much longer than the short local trains we sometimes rode around Prague.

"All aboard!" the conductor shouted. "This is the overnight train to Dresden, with a final stop in Amsterdam. All aboard!" Several toots of the engine's whistle signaled the beginning of our journey. Slowly the train pulled out of the station, past the yard full of freight cars, old engines and smaller trains, then past a big church and my last view of Prague Castle. As the train wound its way out of the town, it gained speed.

The conductor came by, checked our tickets and warned us not to open the windows, because the engine spewed a lot of dust and coal that could get into our eyes. More gray smoke wafted outside, blocking my view. My father must have seen my wide-eyed fear and kept reassuring me. "America is a wonderful country. Aunt Mary Anne and Uncle Leo will help you, and I gave them some money to cover your expenses." Father seemed sincere, and I wanted to believe him, but I wasn't convinced. He said he would join us as soon as possible. Then his voice trailed off. No one said much; it was an uncomfortable ride for everyone. America sounded interesting, but I didn't really want to leave Prague. This was where I was born. Did we really have to move? The communists had done nothing to harm me.

In several hours we reached the last station in Czechoslovakia before the train crossed the border into East Germany. My father was not allowed to go further. My parents embraced and my dad gave me a big hug. "Peter, be a good boy and listen to your mother. I love you." And with those words he exited the train. He was leaving my life again, and I didn't know when, or if, I'd see him again.

He waited on the platform as Czech police came through the train.

A young policeman came into our compartment demanding to see our passports and suitcases. He wanted to know where we were going. My mother explained that we were taking the train to Amsterdam and then sailing to New York. The policeman inspected our passports and visas very carefully. I wondered what he was looking for. Then, in a harsh voice, he asked my mother questions about where she was born, when she married and whether she carried any Czech money. The communist government limited the amount of money each person could take out; any excess currency was confiscated at the border. Mother answered his questions, opened her wallet and handed him the paper money she had and a handful of coins. Then he asked to see the tickets for the boat. My mother handed him the tickets and he again took his time looking at them. Was he looking for forgeries? I was getting nervous. What if he just kept the tickets and sent us off the train?

Then he turned to me. He asked where I was born and what grade I was in. I stammered an answer that seemed to satisfy him. Then he turned to inspect our suitcases to see what we were taking with us. My mother had typed a very detailed list of every item we had with us, and handed it to the policeman. She said that we had mostly clothing, a few kitchen items and some books. "Not much, really," she said, trying to force a smile. But her lips remained tight. He pulled a suitcase off the luggage rack and started to open it. Just then another policeman shouted that he needed help in the next carriage. The policeman left the suitcase open on the floor, stamped our Czech passports and handed them back to my mother.

My mother quickly closed the suitcase and asked me to put it back on the luggage rack. She told me to sit down and she sat, too, smoothing her coat and giving me a steady look, as if to say, not a word out of you, understand?

Father was waiting on the platform as I pulled down the window. I told him that it was too bad I hadn't taken the soccer ball with me. This was a coded message meaning that we could have taken a stamp collection, which included some valuable old stamps. Whether or not to take that collection of stamps had, for weeks, been a heated topic between my parents. According to Aunt Mary Anne, the stamps we owned could easily be sold in New York, where there was a demand for European stamps. But my mother was afraid that if the Czech police discovered stamps in our suitcase, we'd be arrested. Father was always more of a gambler than my cautious mother, but even he did not want to risk our arrest.

Dad looked angry and said that he'd bring the soccer ball with him. As the engine's whistle shrieked, I shouted, "Hope to see you soon." I waved goodbye, and as the train pulled out of the station, my father became smaller and smaller.

Finally I could no longer see the platform where he stood waving. Instead of crying I thought about the stamps we left behind. It seemed easier to worry about stamps than about my father. We could not have guessed that a policeman would not fully inspect our luggage. Even if the best stamps had been sewn into the lining of the suitcase, he might have found them. I kept thinking about what could have happened, until mother interrupted my fantasy.

She placed her arm around me and reassured me that my father would join us as soon as he could. Then she pulled a sandwich out of the bag, egg salad on my favorite bread. I didn't have much of an appetite, but the smell of the mustard and eggs between two pieces of fresh bread made me take a bite. The lunch reminded me of home, and I washed it down with a bottle of Fanta orange juice, an exotic drink introduced to Czechs by American GIs after the war. The American drink made me think of the journey ahead.

The hectic day and the food made me tired. Soon I was dozing, my head in my mother's lap and my legs stretched out on the seat next to her. The steady clack of the train wheels helped me fall asleep.

I don't know how long I slept, but when I opened my eyes, I was surprised to see the city of Dresden. There were rows and rows of bombed-out houses. The external walls looked as if they had been ripped off, exposing many inner rooms, some intact, others torn in half. Light fixtures dangled in destroyed rooms; bathrooms had no plumbing, only holes in the walls where fixtures should have been, and the doors lay on their sides. Mounds of dirt and debris rose up everywhere. I saw several destroyed rail cars, a mangled German army truck and an overturned streetcar.

I couldn't believe what I saw, and mother's face showed that she was also shocked. I asked her what happened.

She explained that Dresden was heavily bombed by the British and American air forces in February of 1945. My parents had visited Dresden before the war, and mother said it was a beautiful medieval city with gardens, fountains, museums and historic palaces. Her voice quavered as she spoke. She said we were in the railway yard, near the center of the city, which suffered high casualties.

I wanted to know why the Allies wanted to destroy such a place and how many people had died. My mother said that it was wartime and the Allies wanted to beat the Nazis and win the war as quickly as possible. She said that the targets were military and industrial but that at least 25,000 people died, and perhaps more than that. No one knew for sure. None of this made sense to me. I wanted to get away, to get to Amsterdam as quickly as possible.

Had it been bombed, too?

Part III

Life in America

1948-1952

Chapter 26
Big Boat

After a 16-hour train ride, we finally arrived in Amsterdam. The terrible destruction of Dresden upset me, but my mood improved when I saw the large market outside the Amsterdam railroad station, bursting with various foods and colorful flowers. I saw rows of roses, chrysanthemums and other flowers in shades of red, yellow and blue.

I was more interested in the huge circles of cheese on display; my mother said these were wheels of Gouda, the most popular Dutch cheese. In German, she asked one of the merchants about the cheese, and he told her that the largest wheels weighed more than 25 pounds. He offered us a sample, which Mother wanted to pay for, but he waved her off. Edam was the next cheese we tasted, and it came in smaller rounds. A third cheese tasted very smoky. I said "thank you" in Czech because I did not want the man to think I was German. He appreciated my politeness and handed me another slice of the smoky cheese, which I quickly devoured. I couldn't believe the difference between the limited items we had in Prague, even after the war, and the variety of foods, flowers and vegetables at this Dutch market.

The following day my mother and I met a Czech couple who were touring Europe. They had moved to the United States before the war and become American citizens, and the man had served as an officer in the U.S. Army. They rented a car and offered to take us around Holland for the next few days. Because they were sailing back to the U.S. on the same boat as we, they also offered to drive us from Amsterdam to Rotterdam, where we would all board the boat.

For the next few days I was overwhelmed with the sights of this welcoming country—windmills, canals, lots of foods and clean parks. Women and men seemed to wash and clean their homes every day, and many wore wooden clogs, not shoes. My mother was astonished at the variety of merchandise found in most stores. Although Holland had been occupied by the Nazis during the war, we saw few obvious signs of the occupation as we traveled around.

My happy feelings changed on the day we drove from Amsterdam to Rotterdam, a distance of about 35 miles. As we got closer to the city, we saw damaged buildings—homes, office buildings, hospitals and churches. Some of these structures had been repaired, but some were still torn apart, ravaged. I started to wonder why war was so destructive, and why so many civilians were killed if it's soldiers who are supposed to fight wars. I found it all quite confusing and unfair.

I asked the American officer about the war and he said that the port city of Rotterdam was bombed heavily by the

Luftwaffe, the German air force. The German army invaded the Netherlands, but the Dutch army and civilians strongly resisted the attack. What the German army thought would be a quick victory turned into a stalemate. On the fourth day of the German attack, Hitler decided to demoralize the Dutch population into surrender. Dutch resistance had to be broken, and on May 14, 1940, Hitler ordered the Rotterdam Blitz, the aerial bombardment of Rotterdam. Even though the Dutch negotiated a ceasefire, the German air force kept bombarding Rotterdam, destroyed most of the historic city center, killed about 900 people and made 85,000 others homeless. Listening to these terrible details rekindled my anger and fear of Hitler and the Nazis.

The next day we finally boarded the *SS Nieuw Amsterdam.* The ship looked brand new, featuring crisp stripes of red, white and blue, with two huge smokestacks painted in a glistening gray. It had been used during the war to transport Dutch and British troops and had recently been refurbished. Crew members in crisp white uniforms offered smiles and greetings, so unlike the harsh policemen in Prague. One took our suitcases and motioned for us to follow him. We walked down three sets of stairs to the third-class section.

The boat was like a small city divided into three neighborhoods. First class was the most luxurious, and its passengers lived on the top deck. Second class was one flight below, and third class—the least expensive—was barely above the waterline. The ship's rules mandated that 12-year-old boys could not stay with their mothers, so I would have a male roommate.

My mother shared a cabin with a French woman who was visiting relatives in the States. The women communicated in French. I shared a cabin with an older American man who was returning to his home in Brooklyn. When the crewman knocked on the cabin door, the older man, already settled in, looked unhappy to see me. I think he was hoping to have the room to himself; I, too, was not prepared to share a room with a stranger.

The man was Russian by birth, and even though he had lived in Brooklyn for years, his English was not much better than mine. I tried talking to him in Russian, but my knowledge was too elementary. So we used our hands and gestures to communicate. I held up a toothbrush to indicate that I wanted to use the bathroom, or he held up a towel to indicate he was going to wash. We managed to coexist, though I would have preferred to share my mother's room.

Meals presented an opportunity and a challenge. I felt like royalty when we first entered the main dining room. There were many tables and many passengers waiting to be seated; we had to sit at an assigned table. The headwaiter showed us to table No. 15, in the middle of the huge room. He held a chair for my mother and indicated that I should sit next to her. A few minutes later we were joined by a Dutch couple who spoke German, so we could all communicate. Another couple arrived, announcing they were from New Jersey. Their English sounded different from what I heard on the radio from London. Most of the time the adults spoke to each other, but once in a while the gentleman from New Jersey would ask me something I only partly understood.

The table was covered with a linen cloth; a place setting consisted of a soup bowl placed on a large dish, a spoon, two forks, a knife and a fancy water glass. Everything was clean and shiny, with a vase of freshly cut flowers in the middle of each table. I spent most meals observing the scene in the dining room or talking with my mother. My most important conversations were with Walter, our Dutch waiter, who understood enough of my English to know that I liked cake and ice cream. He made sure I got my share for lunch and dinner.

I believe I ate more food during the week we crossed the Atlantic than I had in years. My mother encouraged me to try new things: fish I did not know existed, cuts of beef and sausages I had never tasted. But I had limits. When I tried a forkful of *hollandse nieuwe haring* (pickled herrings with chopped onions), I stopped. Other cold fish were not to my liking, but a dish of mashed potatoes mixed with vegetables and a large *rookworst (*smoked sausage) tasted fine. And the Dutch beef was excellent. The desserts were outstanding: chocolate cakes, fruit tarts and many ice cream flavors. And I learned about new Dutch favorites—*poffertjes* (small fluffy pancakes topped with powdered sugar and butter) and *stroopwafel* (a waffle cookie of two thin layers with syrup in the middle).

During the first few days of sailing, the dining room was full of hungry passengers, keeping the waiters busy. Three full meals were served every day, beginning with a full Dutch breakfast of omelets, ham, fish and cheese. At lunch there were salads, cold meats, more fish and more cheese. The evening meals consisted of three courses: soup and a salad, beef or pork and a lot of desserts displayed on a rolling cart.

There were so many choices, I didn't know what to eat first. Throughout the war we experienced food shortages; there was never enough. During the last two years of the war, most Czechs were lucky to have two meager meals a day. My mother and I had very little meat, poultry, dairy products or fresh fruits. Most foods were rationed. But no such food scarcity existed on this boat. Since my parents had paid in advance for all the meals, there was no holding back. My mother and I were often among the first people in the dining room. But as the sea got more and more choppy and the boat swayed incessantly, fewer and fewer people showed up. My appetite also diminished. My stomach felt queasy, my balance was off and I was either going to my room downstairs to nap or staying on the open-air deck. The man from New Jersey advised me to stay on the top deck as much as I could. I did like the fresh air, and I could see the horizon, whereas downstairs I could feel the ship rolling.

My goal was to eat as many meals as possible. Halfway across the Atlantic, my mother and I were among the few people still in the large dining room. However, the next day I had to excuse myself right after soup. As I was leaving, Walter, our waiter, who could be sarcastic in his humor, told me that the chef would be upset with me for not finishing the meal he so carefully prepared. I didn't think he was funny.

On the top deck I'd look for a spot to read my book about American Indians, written by a Czech author who apparently never left Prague. As I read it, I kept wondering if I'd meet Indians in New York. I also read that there was gold in the streets of New York City, and I hoped to find some.

As we got closer to America, the sea became smoother and life returned to normal. The *SS Nieuw Amsterdam* finally entered New York Harbor on the evening of November 8, 1948. The passengers were encouraged to stand on the top deck to see the skyline of downtown Manhattan. There were many "oohs" and "aahs" as the Statue of Liberty came into view, standing at the entrance to New York Harbor. Her crown was lit up and her torch ablaze; she was a beacon for all. Seeing the full-sized statue in person took my breath away. She was more beautiful than I imagined, her tall and graceful presence so welcoming. My eyes filled with tears.

Manhattan's tall buildings were also lit up with yellow, blue and red lights, some even flashing. The sight was overwhelming. I recognized the Empire State building in the distance. In a Prague movie house, I had seen King Kong climb that building. I was secretly wishing I could see the gorilla climb the building right now. I clutched my mother's hand and thought of the long journey we were completing and the people we left behind, especially my father. The moisture in my eyes was from tears of joy, not sadness. I felt hopeful. It seemed that one chapter of our lives had come to an end and another was starting.

Almost on cue my mother reminded me that today was election day, where Americans had free and open elections. The day we arrived was the day Harry Truman, a Democrat, and Thomas Dewey, a Republican, vied for the presidency of the United States.

Were we finally free?

Chapter 27
New York City

I was so excited after seeing the Statue of Liberty and the skyline of Manhattan that I could not fall asleep that night. I was back on deck early in the morning to look at the skyline again. I had never seen so many tall buildings. They seemed to be so close I could almost touch them. I didn't see any signs of war, no destroyed storefronts or burned-out train cars. It dawned on me that World War II had not been fought on American soil.

It was time to be questioned by the U.S. Customs officers who sat at a long table on the ship with an American flag behind them. A photograph of President Harry Truman hung on the wall. There were no Nazi flags or photos of Adolph Hitler or Stalin anywhere. One of the officers waved to us. It was our turn, and as my mother and I stepped forward, I felt a knot in my stomach. His uniform was similar to that of a Czech policeman. I recalled the nasty Czech policeman when we crossed the border, but this officer was smiling, an expression I'd never seen in a uniformed man. When he asked to see our papers, I tightened up. He quickly glanced at them and returned the documents. With a smile he said, "Welcome to the United States." He never looked at our suitcases. I was expecting another inspection by a second officer, but he just waved us on. My mother and I both exhaled. We had made it to America.

As we walked down the gangplank, I heard the word "Zdenka." I looked around and saw a tall man wearing a hat like my father's and waving to us. "Zdenka and Peter, how was your trip? Welcome to America."

I was finally meeting Uncle Leo Altheim. He gave my mother a hug and extended his big hand to me. My mother thanked Leo and said it was so nice to see him again. She added, "Our trip was fine, but the sea was choppy. The New York skyline is so impressive."

"Welcome, welcome. Peter, are you hungry?" Leo asked, pointing to his stomach. I thanked him in my halting English and said that I had had breakfast on the ship. "No problems on the boat," I reported. "Ah, good," he said, and tousled my hair. "Who needs trouble?" he added and winked at me. I already liked him.

Leo took my mother's suitcase and asked more questions about our trip. We walked away from the dock on the West Side, heading east on 42nd Street. The street was wide and full of shops, movie theaters, restaurants and hotels. As we walked, I saw groups of mounted policemen wearing dark blue uniforms and helmets. Their horses trotted near the curb, right next to the sidewalk. One horse came very close, but the policeman pulled him back. The horse wore blinders, and I wondered if it was scared by cars and trucks.

Some of the cars were painted yellow with black checks and a little box sitting on top. Leo explained that they were called Checker cabs and could carry up to six passengers. He said, "You'll see. We'll take one later." And he laughed again. What a happy man, I thought.

The streets were noisy. Cars and cabs honked their horns constantly. I had never heard such noise in Prague or Amsterdam. Public buses and large trucks competed for street space, and whenever the lights turned red, traffic stopped and exhaust pipes spewed out gray smoke.

My eyes fell on the many blinking neon signs in red, blue, white, green, yellow and brown. "Going out of business sale," "All you can eat," "Big Band music," "Latest electronics," "Come in and look around." There were people everywhere, men in suits and women in dresses and high heels, most walking briskly. Leo explained that most people were going to work in offices or shopping in the many stores in this area.

After a 20-minute walk, Leo announced that we had reached Times Square. I asked why it was called Times Square, and he pointed to the large electronic screen flashing the headlines. Leo said the headlines changed all the time and included politics, business, sports, entertainment, weather, everything. A lot of people were reading the latest news before moving on. The electronic board was owned and operated by *The New York Times*; Leo called it the best newspaper in America.

We took a staircase down into the subway and stopped at a row of turnstiles facing the platform. Leo reached into his pocket and pulled out three round yellowish coins. He said each of us needed one these tokens to ride.

He showed me how to place a token into the turnstile, which I did, but nothing moved. Leo told me to push it, and finally the heavy wooden turnstile turned. There were four thick wooden arms, and when I put the token in the slot it turned a quarter of the way, allowing me to enter. I'd never seen anything like it.

We moved to the platform and waited for a train to the Borough of Queens. I asked whether the Queen of England lived there and he laughed. Suddenly, out of the darkness of the tunnel came two headlights and a train. It was gray and looked dirty. As it pulled into the station, Leo told us to stand back. Everyone got off the Queens train, since this was the last stop in Manhattan. "Peter, let's go to the front car so we can see well." He pointed to a man in a uniform who carried a set of keys and a metal handle. "That's the conductor," Leo explained, as the uniformed man unlocked the door to a small booth and placed the handle into a panel facing the front of the train. Leo explained that it was a safety measure: only someone with the handle could start and drive the train.

The conductor's voice came over the intercom, but the sound was so full of static that I could not understand him. Leo said we were on the No. 7 train about to leave for Flushing. We stood looking down the track. The train started slowly as the lead car hugged the tracks, snaking left and right, and then picked up speed, moving fast, then slowed and came to a stop. "Vernon Boulevard," the conductor announced. At every stop some people got off and others got on. Leo explained that some people work in Queens and others live there. I looked around the interior of the car and saw the woven wicker seats. There were maps of the route in glass cases on the wall and a long metal bar with leather straps hanging down overhead.

"New Yorkers are called strap-hangers because they're always hanging on," Leo said with another smile. Sure enough, as the train sped up more passengers gripped the leather straps. There were also several large metal fans suspended from the ceiling. Leo said they were turned on only during the summer.

Suddenly the train emerged into daylight onto an elevated track. Leo explained that when it was underground, the train was called a subway and when it emerged, it was called the El, short for elevated. In half an hour, we got off at the Jackson Heights stop. This time we took a steep set of stairs down to the sidewalk before walking a few blocks to a large apartment house. We took an elevator up to the Altheims' apartment. Mary Anne was excited to see us. She kissed my mother and gave me a welcoming hug.

"Come in, come in, welcome to America," she said. Mary Anne showed us their comfortable, well-lit apartment. The air smelled of freshly baked muffins. When asked again if I was hungry, this time I replied with a strong, "Yes, please!" It would be my first American meal. For the next few weeks, Leo and Mary Anne made us feel at home. They fed us, showed us around the neighborhood and found a room for us in a nearby apartment house.

I remember my first Saturday in the United States. Leo announced that we'd go to the movies right after brunch. I could not figure out the difference between lunch and brunch. Leo explained that brunch is a meal that combines breakfast and lunch, which I understood when I saw the dining table full of plates piled with food: scrambled eggs, sliced tomatoes, hard cheeses, cream cheese and two items I had never seen.

"These are bagels," Mary Anne said, pointing to round breads with holes in the middle. Some were topped by sesame seeds, others poppy, and one had all sorts of toppings. She called it an "everything" bagel; it was the one I wanted. Mary Anne sliced the bagel in half, spread cream cheese on both halves and then placed several thin slices of something pinkish on top of the cream cheese. She explained that it was smoked salmon. I wasn't sure, but when I bit into it I liked it.

After brunch we were joined by their neighbor's two kids, Sammy and his sister, Maddy. Sammy was taller than I and lean, while Maddy was about my height. Sammy stood very straight and seemed serious, while Maddy smiled a lot. They were around my age, but my English was limited, so we did not talk much. We all set off for the movies, and during the walk Leo told me about Saturday matinees.

When we got to the movie house, Leo bought four tickets. We entered the building and got into another line. When we reached the counter, Leo asked for a large bucket of popcorn with extra butter and four small Coca Colas. I knew what a Coca Cola was but had never tasted one. The drink was cold and fizzy; the bubbles went right up my nose. I liked the taste. Leo told me to take some popcorn, and when I only took one piece, he insisted I take a handful. The butter started to ooze onto my hands and Leo handed me a paper napkin.

The lights went down, and suddenly a group of cowboys appeared on the screen, riding their horses across a rocky terrain. They were headed for a group of Indians sheltered behind rocks and boulders. The cowboys pulled out their pistols and started to shoot at the Indians. The Indians fired back, and pretty soon shots were coming from many directions. The shooting reminded me of the war at home, and I started to look for a spot to hide when Leo reassured me the shots were coming from loudspeakers surrounding the screen. There was a lot of action. The cowboys kept chasing the Indians, who fought back with guns and knives. Several Indians were shot and two cowboys were stabbed. Leo explained, "The cowboys are the good guys, and the Indians want to hurt the cowboys. The Indians are the bad guys."

I flashed back to the toy Indians I had played with in Prague. In my mind those Indians teamed up with American soldiers to fight the Germans. How could my good guys suddenly become the bad guys? The Indians in the film were clever, but also mean. They captured the leader of the cowboys and tied him to a pole. They stacked piles of logs around the pole and set it on fire. As the flames rose higher and higher, the leader was overcome with smoke. I worried that he would be killed. I heard so many gasps, it seemed that every kid in the theater had the same fear. Suddenly the film stopped.

I asked Mr. Altheim why it ended so suddenly. "We'll have to come back next Saturday to find out what happens." He explained that Hollywood made a lot of adventure films called serials, which they divided into segments of 15 to 20 minutes each, and I'd have to come back 10 to 12 times to see it all. He told me the hero always faced danger toward the end of each episode to make it exciting. When I asked whether he meant cereals like for breakfast, he smiled and said, "No, it's spelled with the letter ess." He asked me to please call him Leo, not Mr. Altheim.

I wanted to know why the Indians looked so white, when in my book they appeared darker. Leo explained that most of the actors in Hollywood were white, so the studio made them up to look darker. There was a break so the kids could get more popcorn and soda before the feature film began. I still had plenty of both. The feature film was much longer, with both bad cowboys and good cowboys but no Indians. One tall man wore a five-pointed star on his shirt and was called the sheriff. He fought and killed a number of the bad men. It was all exciting, and I didn't see one Nazi or Russian soldier in the entire film.

I hoped we could come back the following Saturday. Leo said that we could.

Chapter 28
Mother's First Job in America

Mother was a hard worker. She had always seemed to be doing something: tidying the house, food shopping, cooking, washing and drying dishes, mending socks, sewing on missing buttons, dusting curtains, doing something productive. She would not sit down until all her chores were done. She would then step out of the apartment or house for a cigarette, then sit down to read a book.

My mother brought her work ethic to the United States. She believed that the way to succeed in America was to become an American as quickly as possible. Maybe she learned that in France where, as a young woman, she learned the language by living and teaching school in a French kindergarten. I was told that she started to dress like a Frenchwoman and she learned to speak French fluently. Even when she returned to Prague, she would dress that way.

When we came to the United States, my mother's motto was: Learn the language and the customs of America, and forget about Prague.

I believe this is why she applied for a job as a governess with an American family, to learn the language and customs of America. She registered with an employment agency in New York City and asked to be placed in a nice area in the suburbs. She could have found a similar job in Manhattan, but she liked the out-of-doors and enjoyed being around flowers, gardens and trees. She also believed that my life and hers would be safer and more pleasant away from the big city. To my mother, the suburbs were the place to assimilate.

A week or two after we arrived in America, she was offered a job with a family in Long Island, about 20 miles east of Manhattan. Leo and Mary Anne drove us to Levittown on Long Island to meet the new family.

At the end of World War II, GI soldiers returned from overseas, married, and wanted homes of their own in which to raise a family. Responding to this demand, Abraham Levitt and his sons built the first mass-produced planned community, Levittown, in Hempstead, Long Island.

When we arrived my mother and I were welcomed by a young husband, wife and infant twins. My mother and I were offered glasses of water, and then we sat down at the living room table. The husband had to go to his office and excused himself. The wife spelled out what she expected my mother to do. She seemed so young she could have been my mother's daughter.

She had a list of "chores," which started with "taking care of the twins," but she also wanted mother to clean the house, do all the laundry and help with shopping and cooking. As she talked to us, the twins slept in a wide crib in the living room. When they awoke, my mother got up to help change diapers and feed them milk from a bottle.

After a while the wife showed us a room in the basement. I expected a really nice room; this was America. But when the door opened we saw a small bedroom, about the size of Paka's room in Prague. But Paka's room featured a large window looking out at the river, while this one had one small window looking out on the paved driveway. I wondered why my mother only partially unpacked our suitcases. Perhaps she already had some doubts.

It was obvious that the young mother had her hands full with two infants and a busy husband. It turned out that the woman also needed frequent naps, maybe because she was tired or overwhelmed, or both. Caring for the two infants was such a demanding job that little else seemed to get done. The couple expected my mother to do everything, and even though she tried hard to complete the many chores assigned, she simply could not. Even on our first full day there, she fell behind.

Mother was not one to complain. She got up early the next morning and was ready to tackle her chores. She suggested that I explore the neighborhood and find kids my age. I came across some boys who were riding their bikes. I stuck around, and finally one of them handed me his bike to try. For a while we all rode slowly around the neighborhood, but my English was so limited I had trouble connecting with them. When I returned the bike, the kids took off, but I decided to run after them to show what a fast runner I was. I ran so hard I did not see a car coming around a corner and was almost hit. The screeching of the car's brakes scared me. I did not want to get into trouble, so I took off again. Though I wasn't sure where I was, I found my way back to the house.

I know that my mother tried hard to please her new employers. She did not show her feelings, but I sensed that the demands of the job were too much, even for her. I was not surprised when, after four or five days, we headed back to Leo and Maryanne's neighborhood, back to the rented room in Jackson Heights.

I believe the whole Levittown experience embarrassed my mother, who had prided herself on accomplishing many things at once. She tried to be the savior those folks expected and needed, but she probably felt that she had failed. Yet Mother was determined to succeed. The employment agency found another family looking for a governess.

Chapter 29
Larchmont

It was late November 1948. My mother had been offered a new job with a different family, the Loebs, also living outside of New York City. We waited with Uncle Leo and Aunt Mary Anne in front of their apartment building in Jackson Heights, Queens.

A powerful-looking black four-door sedan pulled up to the curb. I learned later that this was the newest Buick model, their flagship, called the Roadmaster. I took in the long wheelbase and fenders that swept back from the front all the way to the rear. A stocky dark-haired gentleman wearing a suit got out of the car, introduced himself as Mr. Robert Loeb and shook hands with everyone. He loaded our two suitcases and several bags into the large trunk of the car. I had the feeling that Mr. Loeb was in a hurry; he didn't make conversation with Leo and Mary Anne.

My stomach started to tighten. I felt scared again, leaving our friendly, newfound relatives. I noticed my mother gripping her purse, something she used to do during the Nazi occupation. We waved goodbye to my aunt and uncle, but I did not want to leave. I wanted to be near them so I could spend time with Uncle Leo and have some fun. Unfortunately, Leo and Mary Anne's one-bedroom apartment was too small to hold us. And Mother didn't want to work in the city; she wanted to live and work in the suburbs.

We sat in the back seat and looked at the narrow streets of Jackson Heights, the long bridge we crossed and a three-lane highway leading out of New York City. It was a silent ride; Mr. Loeb did not speak Czech and our English was limited. After an hour, the car came to a stop in front of a large house. We were in Larchmont, New York. I turned to mother and said in Czech that this must be America, because the house is so huge.

To me it looked like a mansion, with tall columns, a low stone wall around the front of the house and a long walkway made of flat multicolored stones leading to a three-story house. My mother called it a Tudor style. I spotted a basketball hoop suspended from a telephone pole. I yelled "*kosikova*," the Czech word for basketball, which I had learned to play in Prague. I also spotted a huge lawn on the other side of the house. It looked like a park.

Mr. Loeb unloaded our bags and placed them on the sidewalk. He looked annoyed as he pointed to one of the two suitcases, expecting me to carry it. He motioned for me to follow him up the stone stairs into the house. The first room held a large piano, a fireplace, a couch and comfortable looking chairs and a carpet like the one we had in Prague. To the right, a staircase led upstairs. Instead of going up, Mr. Loeb led us into the kitchen, made a sharp right turn, and entered a small bathroom that led into a small bedroom.

"This is your room," he said.

Great, I thought, my very own room right off the kitchen.

I was happy. I set my suitcase down, ready to explore. But then Mr. Loeb brought my mother's suitcase into the same room. I was confused. Why was he putting Mother's suitcase in my room? I saw two single beds with a narrow runner on the floor separating them and a nightstand holding a small lamp with two shades and pull strings. A window at the end of the room looked out at the house next door, and a second window, on the side, faced the backyard. Overhead hung a single light bulb.

My mother said thank you to Mr. Loeb, who disappeared. She did not look at me, just set her suitcase on one of the beds and opened it.

In this big house, I thought, my mother and I have to share a room?

In a few minutes Mrs. Loeb came in. She was smiling and welcomed us with a warm handshake. She was about my mother's height, with dark hair. She spoke slowly and loudly, perhaps assuming we could not understand English very well. I didn't understand much of what she said, but her manner was friendly.

Mrs. Loeb led us into the living room, where she introduced us to her two children, eight-year-old Roger and two-year-old Nancy. Almost immediately my mother sat down on the floor and started to play with Nancy. Nancy quickly warmed up to my mother, her new governess.

Roger invited me to see his room on the second floor. It was full of things: a baseball glove, a football, a basketball, toy soldiers, many comic books and a large carpet with different sports scenes woven into it. I was impressed with the size of his room. It was much bigger than our bedroom downstairs. Sunlight flowed through the windows, giving the room a cheerful light which ours did not have. He pulled out a checkerboard and we started to play. Roger wanted to keep playing, but I was called downstairs to unpack.

My mother and I unpacked and put away our clothes in the one small closet and one small chest of drawers. Mother asked me to step out of the room so she could put on the white dress and blue apron that Mrs. Loeb had handed her. My well-dressed and cultured mother was becoming a maid. The New York employment agency that placed my mother in the Loeb household had said she would be a governess, taking care of Nancy and looking after Roger. But as with the family in Levittown, my mother's duties slowly expanded to include cooking and serving meals, washing dishes, cleaning the house, doing the laundry and shopping for food.

In Prague we had lived in a six-room apartment. My parents had their bedroom, and I had my own room, with a lot of space for toys, clothes and books, like Roger's. My room looked out on the river and a major street, not the house next door. What was I doing here? Why had my parents wanted to leave Prague? Sure, life under communism would be bad, but was this better?

I remember that first night in our shared room, our single beds about three feet apart. Each of us had a small light. Before we turned the lights off, my mother said that she loved me and everything would be all right. As I tried to sleep, I could hear my mother softly crying into her pillow.

Chapter 30
First Day of School

We had arrived at the Loeb home on a weekend. On Sunday afternoon Mrs. Loeb wanted to welcome us with an American meal, hot dogs and hamburgers prepared on an outdoor grill. I was familiar with sausages, but I had never tried an American hot dog or hamburger. We all sat down at the picnic table on the enclosed porch. The table held platters full of rolls, sliced tomatoes, ketchup and mustard and cold cans of Coca-Cola. Mr. Loeb grilled the burgers and hot dogs outside and brought them to the table. I liked all the food and ate everything on my plate. We were also introduced to paper plates and plastic forks, which Mr. Loeb said could be thrown away after the meal; they were disposable. In Prague, we would have saved everything by cleaning the plates and plastic forks, but not here in America.

As we finished the indoor picnic, Mrs. Loeb suggested that she take me to the local grammar school on Monday so I could start my education. My mother nodded her head in agreement but Mrs. Loeb saw that I looked scared. She took my hand, patted it and reassured me that I would like

the school, the teachers and the new kids. She told me
Roger liked the school, and so would I. I understood only
some of what she was saying, but I understood the main
message: "You are going to school Monday morning!"

What's the rush? I wondered. I had not been in a
classroom for two months. I kept thinking, why couldn't
I stay home, learn English, read a few books and go to
school later? But I didn't know how to say that in English,
and anyway, Mrs. Loeb was now in charge.

Early Monday morning, three of us—Mrs. Loeb, Roger
and I—piled into Mrs. Loeb's Chevrolet for the short drive
to school. Murray Avenue Grammar School looked very
different from the tall, narrow and gray school building I
attended in the middle of Prague. This school had only
one story and occupied a lot of land. We passed a playground on one side of the building and several sports
fields on the other. Mrs. Loeb parked and we all walked to
the school building. Roger went to his homeroom, while
Mrs. Loeb and I entered the principal's office.

"What is principal?" I asked in almost a whisper, my
voice dry.

"The principal is the head of the school," Mrs. Loeb
told me. "Her name is Mrs. Long."

When Mrs. Long greeted us, she extended her hand.
She was a short woman with dark curly hair and a warm
smile. She invited us into her office, which had a desk
piled with papers and a lot of books all around. The direc-
tors of the two schools I attended in Prague were both
men, wore suits and did not shake hands with their students. Mrs. Long seemed friendlier, but I was still nervous.

"Please sit down," she said, smiling and pointing to wooden chairs on the other side of her desk. She pulled up a chair and sat next to me. "Peter, how was your trip from Europe? And what do you like to do outside of school? Do you like sports?" I understood only part of her questions and tried hard to answer. I wanted to talk about Prague, the train and football but could not do so. Only broken phrases came out of my mouth.

After a few minutes, she and Mrs. Loeb began a conversation in English that I couldn't follow. I learned later that Mrs. Long said I needed to learn English first and that I should be placed in the sixth grade even though I was old enough for the seventh. She also said that I would have to pass an English test before being accepted into the seventh grade, which was part of the junior high school in the next town, Mamaroneck. But I could be accepted immediately as a sixth-grader at the Murray Avenue School. It probably seemed easier for Mrs. Loeb to enroll me closer to home. I could walk to school and learn English. Mrs. Loeb said she would speak to my mother and get back to Mrs. Long the next day.

In a few minutes, Mrs. Long took me to a sixth-grade classroom. The teacher said hello and introduced me to the other kids. She walked me to a desk in the row closest to the window and handed me a math book and some paper.

So, I thought, here I am in an American classroom with a lot of kids. I hope they are nice to me. Can I do the math?

The math lesson was multiplication and division, which I had learned in Prague, so I was able to follow the lesson. The teacher walked around the room looking at the students' work. When she looked at my notes, she saw I had the right answer. She asked me to write my solution on the board. When asked to explain how I got that answer, I explained in broken English that I did all the computation in my head the way I learned it in Prague. But the teacher insisted that I show all the multiplication and subtraction on the board. She kept saying to "show all the steps." I did not understand what she wanted. I had the right answer. What was the problem? The teacher asked another student to come to the board. Everyone saw that I couldn't do this the American way. I returned to my seat feeling confused and stupid.

Lunch was next, and the teacher asked Eva, another sixth grader, to walk me to the cafeteria and help me get lunch. It turned out that Eva had also been born in Czechoslovakia, so we spoke Czech on the way. She showed me the food choices. There was a hot meal of spaghetti and meatballs and broccoli, or a cold sandwich, ham and cheese or peanut butter and jam. I asked for peanut butter and jam, which I had tried the day before at the Loeb house and liked. I think I had encountered enough new things for one day.

Eva was helpful but did not seem comfortable escorting me around. She kept looking around for her girlfriends and kept her distance. Maybe a 12-year-old girl felt awkward being with a 12-year-old boy. Or perhaps she did not want her position as one of the brightest students in the sixth grade undermined by an odd-looking guy. I looked different, wearing an Eisenhower jacket and knickers. I think she felt embarrassed having to walk around with me.

We never developed a friendship. Later my mother learned that Eva's father represented the new Czech communist government at the United Nations in New York City. Perhaps the fact that my mother and I had fled the Communist regime was awkward for her family and they asked their daughter to stay away from me. Whatever the reason, I had the feeling that she wanted to avoid me. The next fall, in the seventh grade, Eva was in the top homeroom, while I was in the slowest.

There were two more classes after lunch, English literature and biology. I was quite lost in the English class and had a hard time following what was going on. The biology class was better because I had a biology class—plants, trees and birds—in Prague. But, again, I could not follow the instructions in English. I found myself looking at the clock, wishing the time would pass so I could get out of this place.

The last period of each school day was gym. In Prague "gym" meant "gymnastics": floor exercises, jumping on the pommel horse, parallel bars and rings. But in Larchmont gym meant baseball, a game I had never seen or heard about.

"Come on boys, move it," the gym teacher shouted. We all ran to the baseball field where we formed a circle and started counting off: one, two, one, two, one, two. The ones ran onto the field, the twos lined up around the wire backstop. Most of the boys had brought their baseball gloves to school. The gym teacher handed me a glove that he placed on my left hand and pointed in the direction of the outfield.

I understood when he told me to catch any ball that came my way. "OK," I answered. It was one English expression I understood. But I must have looked confused. The teacher yelled to a boy named Shimkin to show me where to stand.

Outfield? Infield? Batter? Pitcher? I had no clue what any of this meant. I just tried to follow orders from the teacher.

One boy had a stick in his hands, which they called a bat, and another boy called a pitcher threw the ball near him. The boy swung the stick and missed. Then the pitcher threw the ball again, and this time the first boy hit it and ran to one of the bases. A second boy from the batting team took the stick, and the others were yelling, "Hit the ball." He did, and he ran to the first base, because the previous batter had moved to another base.

I was trying to understand the game while it was quiet in my area in right field. But when the third batter swung the bat, I could see the ball coming my way. I remembered the teacher's order to catch it. I started to run, kept running, stuck my glove out and found the ball in my glove. The boys on my team seemed surprised that I caught the ball. The teacher ran out on the field, shouting. "That was a great catch, Stein, but you've got to stay in right field. You are on the pitcher's mound!" I was confused again. What was the problem? I caught the ball!

One kid came up to me after the game and said his name was Dave Klein. His parents lived near the Loebs, so we walked home together. Dave tried to explain that in baseball, each player has a position and must stay in his assigned area. One player can't run into another player's space. I understood only part of what he was saying, but I realized that soccer, which I played in Prague, had similar rules about players staying in their own area of the field.

When we got to Dave's house, his mother offered me milk and cookies. I never drank milk in Europe. There was very little of it; my parents used it only with tea, and we had no refrigerator to keep it cold. Mrs. Klein placed a plate full of freshly baked chocolate chip cookies in front of us. She said they were David's favorite. "Thank you," I said as I bit into the tasty cookie. And it went well with cold milk. She asked me how I liked America. "Fine," I answered, knowing that sometimes it's better not to tell the full truth.

Outside in the front yard, Dave showed me how to throw a baseball. He helped me place my fingers on the red seams and throw it. Then he took a few steps back and told me to throw the ball at his glove. "Aim at the glove," he kept saying.

We spent about a half hour practicing the throw. Some of my throws sailed over Dave's head, but I kept getting closer to his glove. He showed me again and again how to throw the ball and how to use the glove to catch a baseball; I wondered how long it would take me to learn. Dave threw the ball hard and it stung my hand, but I was determined to learn American baseball. Dave's mother came out to remind him that he had homework. She ushered her son into the house and then drove me home, a short ride to the Loeb house, my new home.

Chapter 31
Eisenhower Jacket and Knickers

What to wear to school became another challenge. After the war I saw American GIs in Prague wearing Eisenhower jackets, which we called Ike jackets. It was named after the popular Gen. Dwight D. Eisenhower, the supreme commander of the Allied Expeditionary Forces in Europe during World War II and later the 34th President of the United States. He had found an earlier uniform too restrictive and wanted a shorter jacket that would be more comfortable and good looking. The Ike jacket became standard issue for U.S. troops.

To me, the jacket looked sporty and I wanted one. I kept badgering my father until he agreed to get one for my trip to America. We went to a tailor in downtown Prague who made the Ike jacket in a tightly woven dark blue gabardine. The tailor added a pair of knickers to the jacket. I liked the way I looked in the suit, smart and grown up. *"Tatínek to je moc krasný. Dekuju mockrát!"* (Dad, this is great. Thank you so much!) I was proud of my new uniform.

I wore that jacket and knickers every day during the trip from Prague to New York. The knickers were fine in Holland and on the steamship, but not in an American sixth grade. From the first day at Murray Avenue School, I got a lot of stares and strange looks. I was the new kid, and the occasional giggles made me feel worse. I think my European outfit was part of why Eva felt awkward walking around the school with me.

The third day of school was really bad. One boy snapped that his grandfather wore knickers. Another asked me if I was a German, and his friend mumbled, "Hey, the war is over. Don't you know?"

By the time I got home from school, I was crying. I told my mother that I felt stupid in the suit. I complained that the kids were making fun of me. Mother tried to console me by saying the suit was handsome and well-made just for me, but I kept complaining. "They've never seen a kid in knickers or an Eisenhower jacket," I said in Czech. "Knickers are for old men, they said."

Mother told Mrs. Loeb, who said she would take us shopping to an Army & Navy store in New Rochelle, where prices were lower than in upscale Larchmont. The Army & Navy store was on Main Street, and we were greeted by a salesman eager to help. He said they had a lot of boys' pants and showed us around the store. He pointed to khakis, blue jeans and dress pants. He saw my "spiffy" knickers and wanted to know where I had gotten them.

I didn't think the salesman's interest seemed real, and I thought he was just trying to make my mother feel good so she'd buy something. But he measured my waist and inseam, went to the back of the store and came back with several pair of khaki pants and jeans. As soon as I put on the new pants I felt better, more American. Mrs. Loeb said that the fit was good and my mother agreed. The salesman also suggested a shirt to go with the pants, and he brought out a pile of shirts, all sporting the label "Made in the USA." We selected a shirt to go with the pants. Mrs. Loeb suggested that we also get a pair of jeans. I was happy, but my mother must have spent most of her first paycheck on my new clothes.

Chapter 32
Shame

At school I was bombarded with questions: "Where are you from?" "Where do you live?" "Who's your mother?" and "Where's your father?"

I did not know how to answer, how much to reveal. When I told a couple of the boys what my mother did, they laughed because she was a maid. One kid told me that his maid was black and that he'd never heard of a white maid. I felt that I was odd and did not fit in. And then I started to feel ashamed of my mother.

This would not have happened in Prague, where my parents were well off and lived comfortably. They had a solid middle class existence; they owned a car, took vacations out of town, swam at a local swimming club and attended the theater and concerts. My mother was employed for most of her adult life as an elementary school teacher, a translator and an office manager.

Suddenly she was no longer middle class but worked hard at a low-paying job for which she was overqualified. Overnight she had become a governess for two children and a maid for a family of four. She was expected to work five and a half days a week. She was off on Wednesdays and half a day on Sundays. On Wednesdays, she'd often take the train from Larchmont to New York City to visit Mary Anne and Leo in their store on Fifth Avenue or to have lunch with a Czech friend or—her favorite activity— visit one of the many museums in Manhattan. I imagined she felt like a European again, seeing the modern art and the latest fashions on Madison Avenue. On some Sundays she and I would take the train to the city, or we'd go for a walk and a picnic or take a local bus to one of the bigger cities in Westchester County, like White Plains or Scarsdale. Most people in Larchmont drove a car and very few took buses, especially on Sundays. Several times, while we walked rather than waiting for a bus, people pulled over to ask if we wanted a ride. That was nice, but I felt that my mother and I were different from everyone else—we could not afford what other folks owned and there were only two of us—there was no husband or father with us.

My mother's birth name was Zdenka, but she decided to use the English equivalent, Helen, when she arrived in the United States at age 44. She spoke with an East European accent, but her years in France had softened its harshness. She spoke French and German, but in Larchmont she had to learn English.

Every night, after her work was done, she would sit at the kitchen table with a cup of tea and study her English grammar book. A small Czech-English dictionary was her constant companion. I would often join my mother and sit at the other end of the kitchen table doing my homework. Sometimes she'd ask me about the meaning of a word and I'd be glad to help. I liked this time with my mother.

In school and the neighborhood, I was the kid who spoke broken English and had trouble understanding. But as my English improved, I became more accepted by the boys in school and started to make friends. As the year progressed, I began to feel more like an American. I began to feel a distance between the new me—the American trying to fit in—and my mother, still a Czech, and who, in my eyes, did not fit in.

Somewhere along the way, I began to resent my mother's accent, her non-American ways and the maid's uniform she had to wear. Being with her did not fit my new image of myself. Making new friends became more important to me than being a loyal son. But I also felt ashamed for having these thoughts. How could I reject the mother I loved? I was reluctant to introduce her to the guys I played ball with. I knew that some of them lived in fancy homes with manicured lawns and private swimming pools. Many had African-American servants. These black women were called maids; the Loebs called my mother their governess, but she was really a maid, an inferior person.

All the boys in the neighborhood, myself included, played baseball and tackle football on the Loebs' big lawn or basketball in the street. After playing outside we were thirsty and stormed the kitchen. We sat down at the large table on the porch and expected to be served by the maid, my mother. I felt uneasy and wondered if my mother sensed it. Sometimes I ignored her and did not even introduce her. I wonder now how painful that was for her.

But one afternoon, after we played on a muddy field, Ross Cleaver had to use the downstairs bathroom and left chunks of dirt all over the carpeted floor. My mother tried to clean the mess as best she could, but when Mrs. Loeb saw dirt on her carpet she was upset. She announced a new rule—everyone had to use the back door and take his shoes off. Roger tried to protest but got nowhere. We had to tell the boys about the new rule. No one liked it. Ross, often wearing socks with holes, became the brunt of jokes.

My mother would greet the boys at the back door, and eventually she learned all their first names. She would bring out milk and cookies she had baked for everyone. When the boys thanked her, she'd say "Velcome." A few giggled at her accent. But I changed the topic when the boys asked questions about her. Once when a new boy joined us, I pretended not to know my mother—I ignored her. Later I felt bad about what I had done.

Why was it more important for me to be part of the group than to respect my mother? I was sorry that my mother had to work so hard, but I also kept my distance in front of the others. It was as if there were two of me: the privileged son who was self-absorbed and the dutiful son who loved his mother, especially when no one else was around. I did not like what I was doing and feeling, but I wanted to be accepted as one of the guys.

The first year or so was difficult, because I sometimes did not know what was happening. Many kids spoke, and their odd expressions made it hard for me to understand. The kids expected a fast reply, but I was usually busy translating their questions into Czech and then trying to answer in English. This slowed me down in the classroom, the cafeteria, in hallways and on the playground. Once I was invited to a new friend's house and misunderstood the day I was supposed to show up. Another time some girls invited me to sit at their table in the cafeteria and I misunderstood what they wanted. Sometimes I looked slow and stupid, and I also felt that way.

I tried several things to improve my English. One was listening to the radio, especially programs like *The Lone Ranger, The Adventures of Superman, Mr. Keen: Tracer of Lost Persons* and *Jack Armstrong: The All-American Boy.* Uncle Leo suggested I start to read comic books like *Superman, Batman, Captain Marvel* and *Wonder Woman.* At first it was Leo who bought me the comic books, which then cost 10 or 25 cents each; later I bought my own. The kids in the neighborhood exchanged comic books, a sort of lending library. I especially liked Superman, because he did amazing things, was very strong and fought Nazi and Japanese soldiers.

The following year I went to Mamaroneck Junior High School for seventh grade. I had the good fortune to be assigned to Mrs. Helen Murray's homeroom. She taught English, literature and social studies. Mrs. Murray was a kind and supportive teacher who believed that everyone's English could improve if they read aloud. One day in class we were told to take turns reading a passage from an adventure book. As the students started to read, I tried to count ahead to see which paragraph would be mine. I was getting more nervous as my turn approached.

It was time to read: "John saw the windy—"

Mrs. Murray corrected, "winding."

"—road ahead. His hears—"

Mrs. Murray, "his horse."

"—was tired from de—"

Mrs. Murray, "the."

"—long trip."

I was turning redder and redder as I heard a few giggles.

"Good job Peter. Keep going, please."

"The ski ('sky') was setting down in the herzon ('horizon')."

I kept reading. "Suddenly, shits rang out."

The entire room burst with laughter as Mrs. Murray tried to gain control, quieting everyone. She said that I was learning a new language and that we all make mistakes. Then she called on Cathleen to read. I learned the meaning of that last mispronounced word right after class.

Mrs. Murray also taught social studies. When we learned about the Seven Years War between Great Britain and France, which was also called the French and Indian War, she asked each student to write a report about the battle of Montreal. The French forces, after losing Quebec, retreated to Montreal. The English forces advanced toward Montreal with more than 17,000 soldiers, while the French were down to about 2,300 men. The French surrendered. Every student wrote about the winning side. I was the only one who wrote about the losing side, the French soldiers and settlers who lost. I'm not sure why I wrote about the French; they seemed more interesting. I often wrote about the weaker side. Maybe my experiences during the war made me identify with the underdog. Even today, when watching sports, I often root for the underdog.

With Mrs. Murray's guidance, I became increasingly comfortable with English. At home Mrs. Loeb sometimes helped me with homework. And on some weekends Mr.

Myer, Mrs. Loeb's friendly father, turned on the radio in the den, and we'd listen to the political news together and talk about it. I never felt this was a lesson but rather a conversation between two persons interested in the news.

Each day I was surrounded by people who spoke only English. Today that method of learning is called language immersion. I don't know exactly when I stopped speaking and thinking in Czech; it just happened over time. Even with my mother, I spoke less Czech and more English. By the time I reached the ninth grade I'd forgotten much of the Czech I had known.

My mother encouraged me to learn English as fast as possible and to learn it well. She also had to learn English to communicate with the Loebs, with Nancy and Roger, with guests, neighbors and in stores. Most evenings around nine, after a long workday, my mother would make a cup of tea. I would sit with her and have a glass of cold milk and cookies. She would ask me about my school day, about the neighborhood boys, how I was. Sometimes she would tell me about her day, but often we just sat at the kitchen table reading *The New York Times* or the *New York Post*, newspapers Mr. Loeb brought home from the office. Both of us learned English, but my mother never lost her European accent, while I was determined to lose mine. Eventually I did.

By contrast, cousin Robert came to America at age 15 and held onto his light Czech accent. It seems that children who learn a language before puberty do so without a foreign accent, while those learning a language past puberty can master syntax and vocabulary but usually retain their accent.

One day in the seventh grade, we were given flyers announcing parents' night. At first my mother did not want to go, perhaps not to embarrass me or herself. She asked Mrs. Loeb to go instead, but Mrs. Loeb encouraged mother to attend. She offered to drive us to the school and wait until the event was over. My mother put on a fine European dress and a hat to meet Mrs. Murray, my home-room teacher. I was nervous about her meeting my foreign-looking and sounding mother. But my thoughtful mother brought a bouquet of flowers for Mrs. Murray, and the two women, both mothers, exchanged family stories. Mrs. Murray became interested in my mother's wartime experiences. They developed a friendship and had lunch together at the end of the academic year. This experience encouraged me to see my mother as Mrs. Murray saw her: a well-educated, interesting and caring person who worked hard and loved me very much.

About a year later things changed dramatically. One evening, after she finished her chores, my mother told me that she had to see a doctor in New York City. She had not had a physical examination since we left Prague some years ago, and it was time. When I asked for more details, she said only that she might have to stay overnight for a day or two and then come back.

It sounded reasonable, so I stopped worrying. But when she didn't return in a few days, I asked Mrs. Loeb what had happened. Mrs. Loeb said that she visited my mother in the hospital and that she was all right but had to stay for a few more tests. When I asked to visit, I was told no, because the doctor ordered my mother to rest and not have any visitors.

I missed my mother but kept busy with schoolwork, and Mrs. Loeb kept reassuring me that my mother was all right. I was a self-absorbed 14-year-old and stopped questioning. It may have been a full week before my mother returned, looking fine. I learned more about her illness only years later. The doctor in the New York hospital had diagnosed breast cancer and told my mother that she needed surgery immediately. That's why she stayed in the hospital and why Mrs. Loeb visited a few times. My mother was a very private person and probably felt awkward talking to me about breast cancer.

After the surgery Mother had periodic follow-up visits with the New York doctor, but she never told me what he said. Fortunately, the procedure had been successful. My mother lived until the ripe age of 99.

Chapter 33
Touchdown

I made friends through sports. Dave Klein, a good athlete, introduced me to baseball in the spring of my first year in the U.S., and in the fall, he introduced me to the American game of football. For me American football was a confusing sport. The name was different: in Prague we played football with a round ball that we dribbled with our feet and kicked into a goal. In the States that was called soccer.

Then there was basketball, which we played almost anytime, even in light rain. Mr. Loeb had someone put up a backboard and a basket with a net on the telephone pole on the corner of his property, and Crescent Road became our "home" court.

We spent a lot of time in the Loebs' large backyard. It became a football field or baseball field, or just a place to hang out and horse around. They let us use the backyard for our games as long as we did not damage any of Mrs. Loeb's flowers and plants and included Roger in our games, which we did as often as possible.

The problem was that Roger was nine years old, and

most of the other boys were 11 or 12. Roger was a good athlete, so we would include him in softball and basketball, but his mother was afraid he'd get hurt if he played tackle football. That did not stop Roger from whining. We would try to include him, especially when we needed another player to make the teams even, but the team that got Roger did not like that solution because he could not cover the taller receivers. So the choice was to include Roger or deal with his whining. Either way I found myself conflicted. If Roger got hurt, it would be my fault. And if Roger did not play, I knew he'd complain to his mother that I kept him out of the game, and it would be my fault. I was relieved when Roger was not around.

Our neighborhood group of about six or seven boys expanded when Jim Bartlett arrived from Florida. Jim played many sports well and was taller than most of us. One day I was in a huddle as Jim, our quarterback, called a play. On his "hup hup hike," Dave, playing defense, came charging at me, pushed me to the ground, and went after Jim. I was stunned: Why had he pushed so hard?

As Jim got up off the ground, he was not pleased. He looked right at me. "Blocking is important and you need to step up." I did not like being criticized in front of all the other guys, but that's the way it was.

After the game I asked Dave to show me how to throw a football. "Pete, grip the ball, find the laces, put your fingers on the laces, cock your arm back and throw the ball." Throwing this odd-looking leather ball was complicated. Many of my throws wobbled and went in different directions. Dave and I practiced a lot before I finally got the hang of it. And, of course, catching the ball wasn't easy either, especially when thrown hard by a player with a strong arm like Jim or Dave.

There were other skills to learn, especially tackling bigger boys. On one play, when I tried to tackle Ross, who was stronger than I, he extended his arm and shoved me in the chest, a stiff-arm. I wasn't hurt, but I hit the ground in a muddy part of the field. When I got up, my hands were covered in mud and my pants were wet.

A few days later Ross gave me a copy of a football magazine with a lot of photos and useful tips. The school library had books about the sport, and I found one called *Football Made Easy*, perhaps an early version of the *Dummies* series of books popular today. I found I liked to look at diagrams of plays and plan ones we could use. With a lot of practice in the Loebs' backyard, often with Roger, I got better at playing football. In the huddle one day, I announced that I had a play. Jim, our leader and quarterback, agreed to try it. I told him the play: fake a pass to Roger, then fake to Ross and hand me the ball for a run up the middle. He called my play, and as I got a block from Ross, I cut right and sprinted all the way for a touchdown. I felt proud that my play worked and wished my dad could see me; he'd have been proud, too. His son had learned to play an American game.

Chapter 34
Becoming Assimilated

When my mother and I arrived in Larchmont, New York, I was confused about who I was and who I would become. I felt my identity shifting from a Czech boy who made it through the war to becoming an immigrant in a new world. Who was I exactly? Someone who had left his home for some reason that I could not clearly explain. Perhaps life in Prague would improve and we would go back there. Why did I have to learn English if we might go back home? Or would my father finally come to the U.S.? Would my mother always take care of other people's kids? Would we have our own home again?

I was a young boy fleeing communism and seeking freedom—was that an identity? Was that enough of an identity? Would there be a time when I would no longer be an outsider and pass for an American?

And what about my religion? I was educated in Catholicism, but somehow, I never fully believed I was Catholic, nor did I really practice it. I don't remember going to church on a regular basis in Prague, although our school class was trained for confirmation. During the war, my parents never spoke about the fact that my father, aunts, uncles and grandparents were Jewish. It was a forbidden topic, too dangerous to talk about. By the time the war ended, any relatives who could have introduced me to Judaism were gone. My father and mother were too busy surviving and trying to protect me. During the war life seemed to be lived day to day and week to week—no one seemed to make long-range plans or have the time to worry about the meaning of life—our goal was to survive.

During my years in Larchmont, I felt my Czech identity slipping away. At first I did not want to let go. I followed news from my country whenever I could, searching for stories about Czechoslovakia in *The New York Times* or the *Herald Tribune*. The summer Olympics were held in Helsinki, Finland in 1952, and I followed the achievements of Emil Zatopek, a Czech long-distance runner whom I had once seen race in a meet in Prague. When he ran he seemed winded, as though he might not finish the race. But he also had a terrific sprint, which he used to win. In Helsinki, he became the only athlete ever to win the 5,000 meters, 10,000 meters and the marathon in the same Olympics. I felt great pride reading about his accomplishments. I also followed the Czech tennis player Jaroslav Drobny, who won the U.S., French, Australian Opens and Wimbledon while also playing ice hockey for the Czech national team. I was thrilled when I read that, like me, he defected from the communist regime.

I knew my father was as proud as I about the achievements of Czechs, but no Czech citizen was allowed to mention Drobny's name in any letters because he had defected to live in Egypt. Dad usually did include some news about my two favorite Prague soccer clubs, Sparta and Slavia, and about the weather, but not much else. It was enough to reinforce my Czech pride while I continued to think of myself as a Czech living in America.

Sports kept me tied to my Czech heritage, and sports also introduced me to an American identity. With guidance from Mrs. Loeb's father, I regularly read the sports pages of the newspaper—baseball, football and basketball were irresistible.

Sometime during the seventh grade at Mamaroneck Junior High School, I began to realize that there was a pecking order in school—the smarter, wealthier and more popular kids seemed to be in other homerooms, not in mine. To hide these differences many schools named homerooms after birds. We were the Cardinals. Most of the kids in our homeroom were from less affluent homes. Our clothing was less stylish, our shoes more scuffed. There were fewer white kids, more black kids and kids with Italian surnames. And we seemed to have more disruptions and more kids with discipline problems. More of my classmates would be called on the intercom to report to the vice principal's office for "behavior issues."

Several times Mrs. Murray told my mother that she was very pleased to have me in her classroom because I was "so well behaved," a "real gentleman" and "never a discipline problem." I certainly learned to respect authority under the Nazi and communist occupations—you stayed in line, obeyed, and stayed out of trouble, a message reinforced regularly by my mother. In Larchmont I did not question authority, partly because I did not fully understand what was expected and because I was scared to do something bad. As my understanding of English improved, I realized I was better off complying with expectations and not giving teachers trouble. Then I would be complimented and left alone. And I started to like the image of myself as a "good boy" who "stayed out of trouble"—it worked for me. I think in those days freedom for me meant not standing out, not calling attention to myself and thereby being left alone.

It was the supportive and nurturing Mrs. Murray, the seventh-grade teacher, who made me feel increasingly comfortable with English and helped me feel good about myself. I began to feel better about everything, more self-assured. I was now able to express what I meant through writing and speech. That made it easier to communicate with the other kids and eventually to be accepted by them.

I also learned English by watching television and movies. The Loebs were one of the first families in the neighborhood to own a large black and white TV set. I had seen a much smaller, experimental TV set in Prague, but that one had flickered on and off with a fuzzy image. Upholstered chairs and a sofa provided comfortable seating in the Loebs' second floor sunroom, where the TV was installed. Roger and I were allowed to watch only on weekends, if we had completed our homework. But every Tuesday the whole family watched *Texaco Star Theater*, starring Milton Berle, the comedian who joked around with his audience, used slapstick and dressed in women's clothing to get a laugh. He was known as "Mr. Television." Mrs. Loeb liked to joke that she had persuaded Mr. Loeb to buy their first set so they could watch "Uncle Miltie." It was fun to see everyone laugh, even Mr. Loeb, who was usually grumpy.

On Saturday evenings we'd watch another creative comedy, *Your Show of Shows,* with Sid Caesar and Imogene Coca. Sometimes I watched newscasts or live dramatic plays, which helped me learn English. On some weekends, Mrs. Loeb would drive Roger and me to the one movie house in Larchmont for a matinee like the one Leo had taken me to in New York City. Most of the films featured cowboys and Indians, pirates or soldiers. I enjoyed the entertainment and adventure, and I was also learning English. As my English improved I was moved from the slowest academic track to a stronger homeroom for eighth grade.

Over the summer before eighth grade, when I was 14, I started to notice girls. Boys and girls started to go to the Larchmont movie house together. That meant getting a dad or mom to drive us, and some parent usually did. After the movie we'd all go out for pizza or take the pizza to somebody's house. I was learning about life in the suburbs, especially in more affluent families.

One day Dave had exciting news. He said that Jim had invited everybody to his house on Saturday evening. "Jim's parents are going out," he said, "and we'll order pizza and play spin the bottle." I had never heard of spin the bottle, so Dave explained the game. Everybody sits in a circle and takes turns spinning a Coke bottle lying on its side. The spinner gets to kiss the person the bottle points to when it stops. I was trying to figure out how that worked. Kissing girls? Really? Other than my mother and some relatives, I had never kissed a girl.

We knew Jim's basement well because we would hang out there. The room had a ping-pong table, chairs, a sofa and a black and white TV set. On the evening of the party, I couldn't see the stairs to the basement because Jim had turned off most of the lights to, he said, "create a mood." It was too dark for ping-pong or TV.

"Hey Pete, how do you like this setting?" Jim asked. I liked my new nickname; it seemed cool and Jim was definitely cool. Jim had moved into the neighborhood from Florida and was one of the oldest guys in eighth grade. Jim was a such a strong golfer that the Mamaroneck High School's golf coach put him on the J.V. team with tenth graders. Jim was popular with the girls: he was tall and strong, with a mischievous smile. He wore short-sleeved shirts with Hawaiian prints all year round.

After pizza and sodas we folded the ping-pong table and moved the chairs. It was time for spin the bottle, and my stomach was already spinning. A lot of thoughts were racing around in my mind. What if the girls don't want to kiss me? What if I don't do it right? And where do I kiss them? On the cheek? Around the mouth? On the mouth?

Earlier Jim had told me about French kissing where the boy puts his tongue in the girl's mouth and moves it around. It sounded disgusting, and I wondered why anyone would enjoy that. Jim assured me that girls liked it. Jim took charge, and had everybody sit on the floor: boy, girl, boy, girl and so on.

I sat down next to Eileen, a neighbor who lived up the street. She was interested in Jim, but Jim did not seem interested in her. Eileen was a good athlete, tall, and often played basketball with us. On my left sat Marion Schafer, who had recently moved to Larchmont from New York City. She was short, very smart and more sophisticated than most of the other kids. I liked her.

Jim placed an empty Coke bottle on its side in the middle of the circle. Dave grabbed the bottle, gave it a strong spin, and it pointed to Sally Dutcher, a popular and attractive girl. Dave crawled toward Sally, kissed her cheek and returned to his spot. Jim, the troublemaker, mumbled, "That was no kiss." Dave was embarrassed. A few minutes later Marion spun the bottle, leaned toward me and kissed my lips. This is fun, I thought, and then noticed how cute she was.

When I spun the bottle it pointed to Bertha, not a popular girl. I could hear Jim snicker, but a spin is a spin. I planted a heavy peck on Bertha's cheek and returned to my seat. I would never have played a game like this in Prague.

By the time school began that fall, I knew more kids, felt more comfortable and accepted. In September, there was an election for student council, with each homeroom choosing a representative. I was surprised when someone nominated me to be homeroom representative. I received the most votes and felt really good about the victory. When I came home with a note about my win, both Mr. and Mrs. Loeb congratulated me. My mother was proud and Roger was impressed.

The Mamaroneck Junior High School student government met every two or three weeks and discussed items brought up by the principal of the school. The first topic was preparing for the fall dance. We talked about organizing a contest for king and queen of the dance, what kind of music to play and how to decorate the gym. Ninth graders dominated the discussions and topics; they pretty much ran things.

It was nice to be a representative, but the meetings took forever and covered topics of limited interest to me. I became more involved when we talked about charging admission to the junior varsity football games, which I opposed. I suggested that all should be welcome, that there were better ways to raise money for school activities. I was happy when others supported my view.

After each student government meeting, I summarized it for homeroom. It took time to organize a report and to rehearse my presentation. Many of the kids seemed not to care and did not volunteer for decorations or clean-up committees. Still it felt good to be involved. When Jim ran for president of the eighth grade, he asked me to be his campaign manager. We had a meeting with Jim's dad, who was in marketing and suggested we "roll out a campaign" with slogans, signs and a rally. I was really involved, and even though Jim lost to Mike, the captain of the football team, I liked the experience with politics. And I got an early taste for representative government, something neither the Nazis or communists believed in.

Being a part of student government gave me more visibility, and I was elected again by my ninth-grade homeroom. At the first meeting that fall, I was elected class treasurer. When I told Uncle Leo about it, he joked that I was well on my way to becoming chief financial officer of a large corporation.

The summer before ninth grade, I decided to try out for football. Roger was now going into the seventh grade, and we would be in the same school. He kept telling me that I really knew the game and could make the team. I realized I had become a big brother to Roger, who wanted to see me in the orange and black uniform of the Tigers. Mrs. Loeb told me that these were also the school colors of Princeton University.

I was nervous about trying out, because I did not think I played football that well. But Jim also encouraged me. He had played football in Florida and was going to try out for quarterback. In July and early August, the two of us spent a lot of time practicing. I would run out for Jim's passes. Most traveled well above the electric wires that cut the Loebs' backyard in half. But one Saturday afternoon, one of his throws hit the wires, which were shaking. Mr. Loeb came charging out of house. "If that ball hits the wires one more time, this field will be off limits. Now get out of here!" That was the end of practice on Mr. Loeb's property.

Finally, one day in August, I reported for tryouts on the football field. The coach had us run laps around the track, watching us closely. Some of the boys were huffing and puffing, but I liked to run, so laps were no problem. We warmed up by throwing and catching balls until the coach divided us up into offense and defense. He'd throw the ball to a player on offense and shout, "Run with it." I saw Roger talking to the coach, and suddenly I heard "Stein." The coach threw me the ball, which I caught. But instead of waiting for teammates to block for me, I started to run as fast as I could. I outran a number of the kids but was tackled by a gang of defenders downfield. The coach yelled, "Wait for your blockers." But I think my speed impressed him.

At the next practice I was told I made the team as a receiver. When I got my orange and black jersey with No. 28 on it, I felt great. When I got home I spread it out on my bed and just looked at it. I wore it to dinner that evening and would not let my mother talk me out of sleeping in it. The next morning, she ironed my jersey in preparation for the Friday evening game, our first.

I liked being part of the team, even if I spent most of the games on the bench. I was called on to play only when we were winning or losing by a lot. I did catch a couple of passes in a game we won 28 to 0.

My social life continued to improve. Sally and Lynn Morrison were two of the most popular girls in junior high. Lynn was short and Sally was tall. They were in the honors homeroom, played on the tennis team and were cheerleaders for the football team. Both were blondes, wore their hair in ponytails and were attractive. I had met Lynn when we were both homeroom representatives, and one day she invited me to a party at Sally's house. I learned later that many kids hoped to be invited to a party at Lynn's or Sally's houses. It meant you were somebody.

I told Mrs. Loeb about the invitation, and she offered to drive me to the party. She seemed impressed that I'd be invited to the home of such a prominent family. I learned later that the Dutchers belonged to the oldest Episcopal Church in Larchmont, while the Loebs belonged to a reformed Jewish Temple. The two families also belonged to different country clubs, the Loebs to a club with primarily Jewish members and the Dutchers to a golf club that for many years accepted only white Protestants. These were some of the long-standing social barriers in town that I did not know existed but were well-known to most of the families living in Larchmont.

At the party at her house, Sally was a perfect hostess. She introduced me to kids I did not know. She lived in a large house with at least three floors, a lot of rooms and a swimming pool. Her parents greeted everyone and then disappeared. We all went down to the basement, a much larger space than at Jim's house. Kids started to dance: the Lindy, bunny hop, the hokey pokey. A tall tenth-grader got onto the dance floor with Sally, moving to some Latin-sounding music I had never heard. They were doing a five-step move—one step forward, one step back and three steps in place. Sally asked us to join them in learning the cha-cha-cha. Her friend showed us the moves as he counted "one, two, cha-cha-cha," going forward, backward and then "cha-cha-cha." It wasn't complicated, and after a while I got the hang of it. And since everyone was dancing together, it didn't matter if I missed a few steps.

I must have done well enough. A few weeks later, Sally invited me to the Junior League Dance at the Larchmont Yacht Club. The Junior League of Westchester, still active today, was a "women's organization promoting volunteerism and improving the lives of folks living in the Long Island Shore communities."

Sally was an active volunteer in the organization, but her invitation raised some questions. She said the dance was formal and I would need to wear a tuxedo. Most of the boys she knew owned a tuxedo. I asked Mrs. Loeb what a tuxedo was and fortunately she found one in her husband's closet. Alterations by a local tailor made it fit. Mrs. Loeb also found a white dress shirt, bow tie and black dress shoes. I think she was proud that a Jewish boy was invited to the prestigious and exclusive Junior League gala. She didn't tell me until much later that Jews were generally not welcome at such events.

I wondered why Sally invited me to be her date. I had assumed that Jim was her boyfriend. They spent a lot of time together, and she'd wait for him after football games. Maybe he was busy that evening, or he was invited elsewhere by another girl, like Lynn. Or was the joke on me and at the last minute Sally would disinvite me? Was I in over my head?

The Larchmont Yacht Club was a fancy, historic place. I was impressed with how grown up everyone looked. All the girls wore fancy gowns and the guys wore tuxes. There was a formal program where each girl, one at a time, was introduced. There was a sit-down dinner, after which we all got up to dance to a live orchestra. I danced with Sally, while Jim danced with Lynn, his date for the evening, as it turned out. Perhaps Jim and Sally were no longer a couple; I was not sure. I realized I still had a lot to learn about girls and dating. But that evening, I was glad to be Sally's date.

Chapter 35
Searching for a Father

While my mother and I learned how to live and survive in Larchmont, my father struggled in Prague. He lived under the newly imposed communist rule, and we had little communication with him. All letters going into and out of Czechoslovakia were censored by officials and we had to be careful what we wrote. Phone calls were almost impossible to make; they were expensive, monitored and required approval. I couldn't just dial up my father's phone number. Such was life behind the Iron Curtain. The formerly democratic country was now completely controlled by the Soviet empire and the Czechoslovak Communist Party.

I learned not to write to my father about problems. I did not want him to worry, so I reassured him that we were fine and that the decision to come to America had been the right one. But without being aware of it, I was searching for a father. I came to love Uncle Leo, but after we moved to Larchmont, I did not see him very often. Mr. Loeb was in my life, and my mother probably hoped he'd provide fatherly guidance, but he seemed removed even from his own children. He spent little time with young Nancy and not much more time with older Roger. When he got involved, it was usually to make a suggestion or order his son to do something or criticize him. I don't remember seeing Mr. Loeb play with his son, throw a ball or run around with him. I overheard comments about Mr. Loeb's weak heart, which prevented him from being more active.

Mr. Loeb was about six feet tall, stocky, with dark hair, and a mostly sour look on his face. I was not the only person he yelled at. Sometimes he would criticize and challenge his wife; at other times Roger was the target. Roger told me once that he was scared of his father. Mr. Loeb had a bad temper, which seemed to worsen when he drank. He worked for a major liquor company, and the liquor cabinet was full of small sample bottles. Mr. Loeb would often have a glass of Scotch before dinner, wine with his meal and a Cognac or Armagnac later. Some evenings he would pass out on the living room sofa, explaining that he'd had an especially hard day at work.

I also discovered that Mr. and Mrs. Loeb had separate bedrooms. His was between Roger's and Nancy's rooms, and Mrs. Loeb's bedroom was down the hall at the farthest end of the second floor. Once when Mr. Loeb was away on a business trip, Mrs. Loeb told my mother that I could sleep in his bedroom. That's where I found a book by Henry Miller, which had been printed in English in Paris. *Tropic of Cancer*, about Miller's life as a struggling writer in Paris, was published in 1934. It was banned from the U.S. for 27 years. Every night I looked forward to reading about Miller's exciting life among the bohemians. He wrote about the experiences of the homeless, the hungry and the lonely. I found the book provided me with many lessons. It was full of vivid passages describing sexual experiences. I stayed up late some school nights, eager to read the next story. I handled the book carefully and always returned it to its safe place under Mr. Loeb's bed.

Mr. Loeb usually ignored me, but sometimes he'd ask about school and teachers. His conversations at the dining table were mostly about news stories and economic developments. But one evening, right after dinner, he looked agitated and ordered me to follow him to the basement. I expected a problem. He pointed to a pile of papers on the floor. "I spent Sunday afternoon straightening up this area, and you messed it up. You are an ungrateful kid!" he shouted. I tried to explain that most of the papers were baseball cards I had been looking at with Roger. My room was small, so we moved his cards and my cards to the basement card table.

I stammered, "I'm sorry for not cleaning it up. I will not do it again." He was still angry. "I did you a favor and I don't have to give you a home." When he finished I ran up the stairs straight to our bedroom, crying. Fat Mr. Loeb was a tyrant. I wanted my father back so that he could beat up that mean man. I jumped onto the bed and began to punch my pillow.

My mother comforted me, but I wanted my dad. I wanted our family to be together again. After many hugs from my mother, I felt better, and that evening I wrote a long letter to my father. By this point, he had managed to leave Prague and was living and working in the city of Wissembourg, in northeastern France. In the letter, I pleaded with him to come to America soon so that we'd be reunited and we wouldn't have to live at the Loebs'. I hoped to hear that he received an American visa, but unfortunately the quota for Czechs continued to be small and all he could do was to wait. I expected a fast reply and kept asking Mrs. Loeb about each day's mail. She told me to stop worrying, because letters to and from France took a long time. I did not tell her what I wrote.

Father's letters from France changed dramatically, because now he could write honestly about life in Prague under communism. He wrote about being questioned and harassed by the Czech police, who had accused him of trying to sell his property, which was illegal under the communist regime. He wanted to take his money out of the country, but that was not allowed. It must have been a very frustrating time.

Fortunately, Leo was still a part of my life. On some weekends, my mother and I would visit him and Mary Anne. Leo would ask about my experiences, the new school and new friends. I believe he was really interested in what was happening in my life, as a good dad would be. He always offered timely information based on the three New York newspapers he read daily: *The New York Times*, the *Herald Tribune* and the *Post*. We often talked about politics, which I liked to do, and about sports, especially the New York teams, the Dodgers, Yankees, Knicks and Rangers.

I had my first paying job with Leo in their Star Stamp Company store on Fifth Avenue between 42nd and 43rd Streets, across from the New York Public library. Leo and Mary Anne's company sold stamps to customers in the store and through mail-order. The Star Stamp Company existed at a time stamp collecting was very popular; in fact, it was one of the world's most popular hobbies. In the 1940s, 1950s and 1960s, most American high schools had a stamp club and when I was in high school in the 1950s, I joined my school's stamp club.

About once a month, Leo and Mary Anne held a "mail auction" of stamps. They developed a 50- to 60-page catalogue that listed a large number of stamps to be sold. The catalogue described each stamp and had photographs of the most valuable ones. I helped Leo bundle the catalogues and haul them to the post office on East 43rd street to be mailed all over the U.S. Interested customers bid on stamps they wanted to buy and returned their bids by mail.

When the mail came in, I would inspect the postmark on each envelope to make certain they met the bid deadline, open each envelope, and assign a unique number to each bidder, recorded their names and their bids. Then I sat with Leo and Mary Anne as they reviewed the bids and chose the highest bidder. I addressed each envelope to a customer. They double-checked my work, usually praising my accuracy, but they also caught errors I made, mostly in the afternoon, right after lunch when I'd get sleepy.

Mary Anne had grown up in the stamp business. Her father was a major stamp dealer in Vienna between the two world wars, and she knew a lot about collecting stamps and their value. My dad said that she was a smart businesswoman.

I loved her, but she would stay at home on some Saturdays, and I liked those days because I had Leo all to myself. When Mary Anne was in the office, she was all business. There was little chatter; everything was quiet except for the occasional business call. At around 12:30, she would call the deli downstairs and order lunch. We'd break for 20 minutes, eat in the office at the desk and then get back to work.

Leo was different. He was more relaxed, loosening his tie as he entered the office and wearing loose-fitting trousers. He would *kibitz* with everyone who came into the store: customers, the mailman, the UPS guy and the cleaning lady. His laughter was infectious. I liked being with him and I looked forward to our time together. We would start work at 9:30, leave the store around 12:30 to go out for lunch and work again till about 4:30 p.m. I usually went home with one or two twenty-dollar bills, which I would proudly present to my mother as my contribution.

A few times we had lunch at the 42nd Street and Third Avenue location of Horn & Hardart, the first food service automat in the United States. I loved the automat, with its rows and rows of freshly prepared foods sitting on plates in windowed compartments, one on top of the other. Leo handed me a handful of nickels, which I used to buy my choice of dishes. First he pointed to a sign that explained "How the Automat Works. Drop your coins into the slot; then turn the knob and glass door clicks open; lift the door and help yourself." There were so many choices I couldn't decide what to eat. "Peter, you can always come back and try something new next time," advised Leo. I felt more grown up as I mastered the automat.

If we got a lot of work done, we'd walk Fifth Avenue. Leo showed me the stone lions—Patience and Fortitude—

guarding the New York Public Library, or we walked to Rockefeller Center to admire the large statue of Prometheus. In winter we watched the skaters at the ice rink, which in December was just below a huge and fully decorated Christmas tree. Once we walked to the old Madison Square Garden on Eighth Avenue between 49th and 50th Streets for an afternoon practice of the New York Knicks basketball team. Before we went, Leo told me about the team and the players. I had started reading the sports pages regularly and learned the players' names— Harry Gallatin, Dick McGuire, Nate "Sweetwater" Clifton, Vince Boryla and others. Keeping up a conversation with Leo made me feel competent. He told me how proud of me he was as I learned about American culture, whether it was sports or domestic or international politics; Leo pursued these topics as passionately as my father did.

Leo combined hard work with having a good time; he liked to kid around with people, to make them laugh. I also liked his informality and comfort with everyone. Perhaps because he had lost his parents and other relatives in the Holocaust, Leo tried to enjoy the life he had. Humor was his primary way of coping; over the years I copied Leo's style, looking for humor even in bleak situations.

In school I still worried whether I really understood my subjects and whether I was learning enough. But with Leo I never worried; he gave me instructions about stamps in a friendly tone, and I had no trouble understanding what had to be done. It was fun working with him. Mary Anne would get upset if the work did not move quickly enough, but Leo stayed calm and broke up tension with a funny remark or story.

Later, when we moved to Manhattan, I would visit Leo's office regularly, even when he didn't need help with stamps. He always asked me what was happening in my life, and I was glad to share with him news about school, my parents, new friends and, later, girlfriends. He was my second dad, and I loved him.

Chapter 36
Escaping Nazism:
Leo and Mary Anne Altheim

Leo and Mary Anne had no children. Perhaps that was due to the political turmoil in their native Austria, the German occupation and the resulting long separation during World War II, when both escaped Nazi-controlled Vienna: Leo on a ship to China and Mary Anne on a flight to the United States. When I helped Leo in their stamp store, we spoke about a lot things but not much about his family. One Saturday I asked him how he and Mary Anne escaped. He laid out a complicated and painful story.

Mary Anne feared what would happen to Jews when German troops marched into Austria in 1938, the invasion known as the *Anschluss*. Despite the responsibility she felt for her parents and sister, Mary Anne was determined to get away from the Nazis. When an American cousin agreed to be her sponsor, she quickly applied for a visa and booked a seat on one of the last flights out of Vienna. Once the German army occupied Austria, things became much worse. Hooligans and pro-Nazi thugs painted six-sided yellow stars on Jewish-owned businesses. One day her father's business—Ehrlich Stamps, located on a fashionable commercial street in downtown Vienna—was vandalized. Leo told me how every day brought increasing tension and a growing fear among Jewish families and businesses in Vienna.

The anti-Semitism that had existed in Vienna before Hitler had become increasingly oppressive. Mary Anne, sensing great danger, wanted her entire family to leave. But the stamp business was very successful, and her parents did not want to give up their home and comfortable lives in cosmopolitan Vienna. In what must have been painful conversations, Mary Anne's parents believed that life for Jews would be difficult but tolerable. Moreover, Mary Anne's younger sister had a debilitating physical condition, and perhaps the parents' feelings of responsibility trumped any thoughts of leaving. Yet, Leo explained, her father encouraged Mary Anne to leave for America.

Leo was also torn. Should he leave with her, or stay behind to help his own parents and in-laws? Leo decided to stay and continue to work in the stamp business with Mary Anne's father. Once Mary Anne arrived in New York City, she kept in constant contact with Leo about the worsening political situation in Vienna. During a tense phone call, she finally convinced Leo to get out. He went to the American Embassy in Vienna but did not have all the papers required for an American visa, so joining Mary Anne in New York was impossible. However, he learned that he might be able to get to Shanghai.

Japan invaded China in 1937, capturing the Chinese capital of Nanking and the port city of Shanghai. The Japanese government controlled the international settlement in Shanghai, called Hongkew, which remained an open city. The Japanese authorities did not require an entry visa or a passport, and these refugees were allowed to settle there.

Uncle Leo said he "ran around Vienna for days" until he found a travel agency that still had a few tickets for a steamship to China. He reserved tickets for Mary Anne's parents, his parents and himself. Leo started to weep when he spoke about how his parents and in-laws refused to leave Vienna. He felt terrible about his inability to persuade them. Leo's parents and Mary Ann's parents and her sister all stayed behind, and eventually all were killed in concentration camps. He felt guilty for the rest of his life.

But Leo was determined to reunite with Mary Anne. He took an overnight train from Vienna to Genoa. There he boarded the steamship Conte Verde for a three-week trip to Shanghai. The boat served fine Italian food and wines and featured live entertainment, but he felt guilty most of the time.

Leo was shocked when he got off the boat in Shanghai. The Japanese authorities ordered all Jewish refugees to live in a designated area, the Hongkew district. It was called the Shanghai ghetto, about a square mile in the poorest, most run-down and overcrowded section of the city. The ghetto held about 100,000 mostly poor Chinese and about 50,000 mostly Jewish refugees from Germany, Austria, Poland, Czechoslovakia and Lithuania, all fleeing Nazi occupation. Leo told me that at first life in the ghetto was bearable because the refugees received food, supplies and financial aid from various international relief agencies, mostly American ones. Despite living in a crowded ghetto, Jewish cultural life flourished. There were schools for children, newspapers, plays and films, and even sport teams for adults.

But when the Japanese attacked Pearl Harbor in December of 1941 and the US declared war on Japan, all outside aid to refugees stopped.

Rumors spread quickly in the ghetto. Leo heard that the Nazis were putting pressure on Japan to deport the Jews living in Shanghai to concentration camps in Europe. However, he read a hopeful story in the local newspaper about the meeting of the Japanese governor with the chief rabbi of Shanghai. According to reports, when the Japanese governor asked the rabbi why the Germans hated the Jews so much, the rabbi replied, "They hate us because we are short and dark-haired." Leo believed that the Japanese leader fully understood the rabbi's answer, and the Japanese kept the ghetto open and, throughout the war, did not arrest Jews.

The ghetto had a curfew, the area was patrolled by soldiers, food was rationed and everyone had to show an I.D. card to enter and leave. But there were neither walls nor barbed wire, as was the case with ghettos in occupied Europe. Most importantly, Jewish men, women and children were allowed to live. Although he was all right, Leo continually worried about his parents and Mary Anne's family. He acknowledged that he was lucky to get to Shanghai because by August 1939 the Japanese did close the city, and no more immigrants were allowed entry.

Many years later, after both Leo and Mary Anne had died, I found a piece of family history that stunned me.

A Boy's Journey

While looking through old photos, I found a package with a familiar label, the Star Stamp Company, 505 Fifth Avenue, New York City, USA. I pulled out about 20 post-marked letters. As I started to read the addresses, my hands began to shake. The letters were addressed to Mrs. Mary Anne Altheim, 40-52 74th Street, Jackson Heights, LI, USA *mit flugpost nach Nordamerika*, (by air mail to North America). Other letters were addressed to Herrn Leo Altheim, 159 Avenue Haiog, flat 137, Shanghai, China (via Siberia). All the stamps were marked *Deutches Reich*. The stamps showed castles and cities, and many had portraits of Adolph Hitler. They were sent in 1939, 1940 and even 1941, and each had a piece of tape across the back of the envelope. On the tape was an insignia of an eagle carrying the symbol of Nazi Germany in a circle with the words *Obercommando Der Wehrmacht* and *Geprüft*—meaning the letter had been inspected by the Nazis.

Then my eyes fell on the return address. Some letters were from Hugo Ehrlich, others from Josephine Ehrlich, Mary Anne's parents. I realized these were the last letters Hugo and Josephine ever wrote. Mary Anne told me they were arrested in late 1941 or early 1942 and sent to their deaths. By 1941 their names on the letters had been changed to Hugo *Israel* Ehrlich and Josephine *Sara* Ehrlich. The Germans forced each Jewish man to add Israel and each Jewish woman to add Sara to their names so that offi-cials would know they were Jews.

Even under the Nazi occupation of Austria and with their impending arrest, Mary Anne's parents had loaded up each letter with as many stamps as possible for their daughter and son-in-law. These were stamps issued by

247

their eventual murderers. I believe the parents, to the end, were trying to help their daughter survive in a new land. They must have believed that these German stamps would have a resale value in the United States and help their daughter financially. When Mary Anne came to New York, she found a job in the stamp section of Macy's department store. The management at Macy's must have been glad to get a new employee who knew so much about European stamps, including those issued by the Nazi regime.

Yet both Mary Anne and Leo held onto those envelopes with the stamps. Perhaps it was a cruel reminder of what had happened to their parents and in-laws. They never sold those Nazi stamps.

I stared at those envelopes with the stamps of Hitler and cursed.

Chapter 37
Reuniting with Father

I did not see my father between October 1948, when I was 12 years old, and April 1951, close to my 15th birthday. It was a long absence for each of us. When Mother and I left Prague, Dad was busy trying to sell an apartment he owned to meet expected living expenses in the United States. But when the Communist Party seized political power, it became very difficult to sell any assets. They imposed strict limits on what people could take out of the country.

Between the end of the war in May 1945 and February 1948, a democratically elected Czech government was in power, and it allowed private property to be bought and sold. The goal of the new communist government which took over the country in 1948 was to nationalize businesses and eliminate private property. Nationalization was the process through which privately owned companies or private assets became publicly owned by the government. Most of the former owners were not compensated for their seized assets.

At home in Prague, Father strongly objected to the new communist-imposed rules and when he was overheard criticizing communist policy he got into trouble. A few weeks after my mother and I left Prague, a policeman appeared at our apartment and ordered my father to bring all of his documents and paperwork to the main police station. He was detained overnight while the police searched the apartment. Father's Czech passport was confiscated, and he was told that it would only be returned once he stopped causing trouble. My father had a tendency to get angry about any arbitrary order, so this intervention by the police was difficult for him.

Without a passport he could not leave the country. Finally, about a year later, he was permitted to leave for France with a note in his document that he was not allowed ever to return to Czechoslovakia. For almost two years he lived in a town in the northeast of France, where he worked for a French bentwood company. After a lot of correspondence and pleading with the State Department, he finally received an American visa in the spring of 1951, allowing him to come to the United States.

Finally, on a sunny day in April 1951, my mother and I travelled to Pier 44 on Manhattan's West Side to welcome him. When he came off the boat, we shared a long, teary hug. When I had left him, my father was a lot taller than I; now I was almost his height. I greeted him in a mixture of English and Czech, but definitely more English. I'm not sure how he responded, but I was embarrassed and ashamed. How did I forget so much of my native language? Was I now an American, no longer a Czech?

My parents agreed that I should complete ninth grade in Larchmont before my mother and I moved to New York City to join him. My father searched for an apartment and found a job in Manhattan while I completed junior high school. I had mixed emotions about leaving Larchmont, a place I had considered home for three years. While I wanted to live with my dad again, I was also anxious about living in yet another new place.

My neighborhood friends, Jim, Eileen, Dave and Marion, organized a goodbye party for me. It was at Eileen's house, around the corner from the Loebs, on a sunny day in June. Eileen's mom baked her fantastic chocolate cake, and the kids all chipped in for my gift: a brand new Larry Doby baseball bat. He was one of my favorite players. Three months after Jackie Robinson broke the color barrier in Major League Baseball's National League, Doby was signed by the Cleveland Indians as the first African-American player in the American League.

I felt sad leaving my friends, not unlike the feelings I had when I left Prague years earlier. I wasn't sure about living in a big city, going to a new school and finding new friends. But we were a family again, and that was important.

Leaving one's home and one's country in the hope that life will be better elsewhere is never an easy decision. Today, so many men, women and children trying to survive in war-torn regions of the Middle East, parts of Africa and Latin America are forced to face that question. Their struggles are documented daily in newspapers and in the electronic media. Similar decisions faced Jewish families as the clouds of World War II loomed: should they leave everything behind and flee, or try to survive under German occupation? As the Nazis came to power, some Jewish families had the foresight and the resources to get out. But once World War II started in 1939, it became almost impossible for Jewish people to leave their homes, as most European countries and the United States refused to accept refugees.

Years ago, when I was a college student, I asked my father how the extended Stein family had dealt with that dilemma. My father's parents and their four adult children, all married with their own families, decided to stay in Czechoslovakia. My father said no one believed things would become so terrible. They all led comfortable lives in and around Prague. My father's parents owned several buildings, and my father owned a factory. Both he and Richard, his older brother, had worked in Germany in the 1920s, and they had German colleagues and friends. His two sisters had husbands whose businesses traded with German companies. Everyone was well-educated and spoke both German and Czech fluently. Germany was a highly civilized nation, and my father believed that the German people would never really elect that "mad man Hitler." He believed that the entire Stein family could put up with the Germans; it would be difficult, but they would survive. He concluded by saying, "How wrong we were, how tragically wrong." Of his immediate family, only he survived.

Chapter 38
Afterword

When in 1993 I answered the knock on my office door and saw the faces of college students who had been confronted by a Holocaust denier, I had no idea that the focus of my personal and professional life was about to change. Would I have become a Holocaust scholar if those students hadn't come to ask for help? Perhaps not. As a sociologist I was actively researching and writing about more contemporary areas of social life, such as dramatic changes in American families.

But the appearance of the students demanded that I look more deeply into the lives of Jewish men, women and children, their families and their communities during World War II. In turn that led me to do research on my parents and their extended families. Trying to unravel what happened to my relatives was personal, and I became more fully involved than I had been with other sociological projects. What would my life be, had the students not sought me out that day?

In my gut I felt that I had a responsibility to act. I realized that anti-Semitism and Holocaust denial existed in my own workplace, elsewhere in the US and globally. I wanted to reach students of all ages and many others through teaching and shining the light of truth, to prevent future tragedies from happening.

As I tried to comprehend the Holocaust, I struggled with my own self-definition as a Holocaust survivor. Years ago, at a conference, I was challenged by several attendees who argued that only persons who survived a concentration camp could legitimately be called survivors. Since I was never incarcerated in a camp, how could I know what happened in the camps? Another person suggested that since my mother was a Christian, I could not be considered Jewish.

Yet over the years of studying the Holocaust and in the experiences of my own relatives, I realized that such narrow definitions are a disservice to the diverse experiences of Jews and non-Jews who opposed Hitler's regime and suffered during the Nazi occupation. In addition to the 6 million Jewish men, women, and children murdered during the Holocaust, about 5 million others were also victims—communists, socialists, priests and nuns, Jehovah's Witnesses, homosexuals and lesbians, Romas (gypsies) and the physically and mentally disabled.

Over the years I've lost touch with the students who awakened me years ago and changed my focus. Inspired by them, I've been busy speaking with middle school, high school and college students and teachers for more than 25 years. In 2014, I was appointed a Holocaust Scholar by the State of North Carolina Holocaust Education Council. With colleagues I've taught a number of teachers around the state and elsewhere. The evaluations have been heartwarming and gratifying.

One teacher recently wrote, "Years ago I attended a one-day workshop at the Museum of the Albemarle where you spoke, and two years ago I attended the Witnessing the Witnesses workshop in Chapel Hill. You were kind enough to send me the slide show you had created. I have used that slide show each year since, and my students find it very powerful and informative. Thank you for the teaching you do."

I strongly believe that all of us need to understand those terrible events of more than 75 years ago, and we must learn, so we don't repeat those tragedies again. In April 2018, *The New York Times* reported on a national survey which found that "many adult Americans lack basic knowledge" of the Holocaust; that lack is highest among people ages 18 to 34. The ignorance is shocking— three out of ten Americans believe that only two million Jews were killed during the Holocaust, and four out of ten do not know what Auschwitz was.

There is some hopeful news: 93 percent of adults believe that all students should learn about the Holocaust in school, and 96 percent of respondents believe this genocide did happen.

Holocaust educators, students and other adults say that nothing compares to the powerful experience of seeing, hearing and reading the testimony of a Holocaust survivor. That is why I continue to speak, teach and write, and why I'm grateful to those students who found me.

Life Remembered in Photographs, Chapters 18 through 38

Chapter 18: Post-War Years

We're finally enjoying freedom.

My parents reunited after the war.

Chapter 19: Catching Up with Father

Father and me after the war.

Chapter 20: A Daring Escape

Three survivors of Auschwitz—Jan Markus, his wife Truda, and
brother Tomas—enjoy life again.

Chapter 21: Fighting in Soviet Union

Survivors: Father's cousin Kurt Fanta and wife Malvinka with our family after the war.

Chapter 22: Surviving Auschwitz

Father's cousin Mana Arendt, who survived Auschwitz, shown with Vera Markus Novak (on right) and my dad.

Chapter 23: Living in Limbo

Charles Bridge and the Old Town Bridge Tower.

Chapter 24: Getting an American Visa

Mother's identity card, in German and Czech, issued during the
Nazi occupation.

Chapter 26: Big Boat

We sailed the SS Nieuw Amsterdam in 1948; it was used during WW II to transport troops.

The Statue of Liberty has welcomed immigrants for decades. Mother and I sobbed as we sailed into NY Harbor in 1948.

We were overwhelmed by the sight of the Manhattan skyline.

Chapter 29: Larchmont, NY

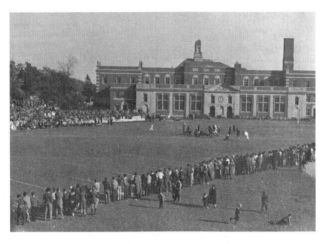

The JV team in action. Photo courtesy of the
Larchmont Historical Society.

Friends at Mamaroneck Junior High School.
Photo courtesy of the Larchmont Historical Society.

Chapter 32: Mother's First Job

Mother was proud to be an American.

Chapter 33: Touchdown

Neighborhood friends introduced me to American football.

Chapter 34: Becoming Assimilated

Photo from my Certificate of
Naturalization, April 1955.

Chapter 35: Searching for a Father

Uncle Leo was a loving substitute father
before my own father returned.

Chapter 36: Escaping Nazism

Leo and Mary Ann Altheim became our sponsors by
agreeing to support us financially.

Chapter 37: Reuniting with Father

Dad arrived in New York from France
in the spring of 1951.

Chapter 38: Afterword

Peter presenting his story to a group of young people.

Discussion Questions for Readers

The following questions can be used with a middle school, high school or college class; a book group; a discussion group or for personal reflection.

1. Peter's relatives faced the question of whether to remain in Czechoslovakia or flee the invasion by the German army. How did they respond?

2. How did Peter's father explain his family's decision not to leave Czechoslovakia?

3. During the war Peter's father would leave home for long periods of time. What happened to Peter's father during the Nazi occupation?

4. After the war ended, how did Peter's father deal with the realization that so many relatives perished during the Holocaust?

5. Some relatives resisted the German occupation. Review their experiences and discuss how brothers Jan and Tomas Markus, Kurt Fanta, Mana Arendt and Leo and Mary Anne Altheim survived the Holocaust.

6. Describe Peter's mother's life during the war.

7. Discuss three ways Peter's life changed during the war.

8. Discuss the differences in the experiences of Peter's Jewish grandparents and Catholic grandparents during the war.

9. Who was Paka and why was she such an important person in Peter's life? Why did she leave Prague at the war's end?

10. There were increasing food shortages during the Nazi occupation. How did Peter's mother and grandmother secure food for their family?

11. During the war the Nazis forced all Jewish men, women and children over age six to wear a badge. Peter's father had to wear the six-sided yellow star showing the German word *Jude* in black letters. How do you think his father felt about wearing such a marker in public? Why did Peter not have to wear the yellow star?

12. How did Peter's life change when the war ended?

13. What happened in February 1948 that dramatically changed his life?

14. How did Peter feel when he and his mother arrived in the US?

15. What problems did Peter face in school, in learning English and in making new friends?

16. How did his mother cope with her life in the US? What hurdles did she have to overcome?

17. How did Peter become like an American teenager? What were the challenges and rewards of learning to be like his new friends?

18. Did you find a central message to the book and if so, what do you believe it to be?

The following ideas are intended to promote deeper thought and discussion of ideas beyond the text of *A Boy's Journey*.

Sociologists who study immigration identify considerations known as "pushes" and "pulls." "Pushes" are factors that encourage people to leave their home for a new country. They include political conflicts and war, ethnic, religious and political persecution and economic problems. The "pulls" are factors having to do with the immigrants' positive expectations of the nations they move to, including the availability of jobs, safety, religious and political freedom, educational opportunities, and, of course, welcoming immigration policies.

1. How do the experiences of Peter's family and relatives illustrate any of these factors?

2. Do you see any parallels between the experiences of Jewish families, including Peter's family at the time of the German occupation, and people fleeing their nations now?

3. Are decisions to stay or leave similar or different from one historical situation to another?

4. Anti-Semitism has a long history. What do we know about the history of anti-Semitism in Europe? How did anti-Semitism grow into hatred of Jews and eventually the Holocaust? Why is anti-Semitism still so powerful today in Europe, the United States and around the globe?

5. How is the continuation and growth of anti-Semitism around the world linked to racism, hatred and oppression?

6. People who practice Holocaust denial reject the historical facts of the Nazi genocide of Jews in Europe. How does Holocaust denial and the denial of other genocides threaten democracy and individual rights?

7. Is there an "immigration story" in your family?

It is difficult to fully understand why the Holocaust happened. In his book *Perpetrators, Victims, Bystanders: The Jewish Catastrophe,* Raul Hilberg suggests that one way to comprehend this tragedy is to identify and name the major groups involved.

- Perpetrators: Hitler and the Nazi Party, police and Gestapo, bureaucrats, German corporations and also other nation's governments and citizens who collaborated with the Nazis.

- Victims: Six million Jewish men, women, and children. Five million others, including communists and socialists, Catholic priests and nuns, Jehovah's Witnesses, homosexuals, lesbians, disabled/ handicapped men, women and children, Roma (gypsies), Russian and Polish soldiers, anyone opposed to the Nazi regime.

- Bystanders: The largest group of bystanders was ordinary citizens who would not get involved in opposing the Nazis. Some governments, churches and organizations also saw what was happening and chose to do nothing.

- Resisters: Brave men and women opposed the German Army. They attacked German troops, blew up supply lines, derailed trains, disrupted communication, rescued and hid downed Allied pilots. Several of Peter's relatives resisted Nazis. Jewish resistance existed in the Warsaw ghetto and in concentration camps, including death camps Treblinka, Sobibor and Auschwitz.

- Rescuers: Men and women who, while risking their own lives, saved Jewish lives. Rescuers included diplomats and businessmen as well as farmers and older folks in rural areas. In a few countries such as Denmark, almost all Danish Jews were saved.

- Liberators: Allied troops—Americans, British, Canadians, French and Russians—who fought and defeated the Nazis and liberated the concentration camps.

Can you apply the same categories to holocausts and genocides that have occurred since World War II, and still occur today?

The bibliography for this book and the following list provide readers with additional sources and resources.

United States Holocaust Memorial Museum, Washington, DC, www.ushmm.org

Facing History and Ourselves, https://www.facinghistory.org

Yad Vashem Holocaust Remembrance Center, www.yadvashem.org

Browning, Christopher. 2007. *The Origins of the Final Solution: The Evolution of Nazi Jewish Policy.* Lincoln: University of Nebraska Press.

Hilberg, Raul. 1993. *Perpetrators, Victims, Bystanders: The Jewish Catastrophe 1933-1945.* New York: Harper Perennial.

Lipstadt, Deborah E. 1993. *Denying the Holocaust: The Growing Assault on Truth and Memory.* New York: The Penguin Group.

Lipstadt, Deborah E. 2006. *History on Trial: My Day in Court with a Holocaust Denier.* New York: Harper Collins.

Acknowledgments

In this memoir I remember and reflect on experiences during the first 15 years of my life. The first 9 years involved World War II. My home town of Prague, Czechoslovakia was invaded and occupied by the German army. Many of my relatives disappeared during what became the Holocaust. When the war finally ended, I lived under communism until I immigrated to the United States at age twelve.

I became a professional sociologist. I've studied and written about human behavior and institutions throughout my adulthood, but writing about my family and about myself has been a new experience. I have recorded my experiences as accurately as possible, with the help of friends and relatives.

Two of my cousins were especially supportive in helping me understand our complex family history. Both of them survived the war in occupied Czechoslovakia, as did I. Vera Markus Novak was born in Kolin, Czechoslovakia in 1926. Her Jewish father, Alfred Markus, escaped the Nazis by fleeing to Shanghai, China, where he lived in the Jewish community. Vera lived in Nazi-occupied Bohemia with her Christian mother, and after the war, she lived with my parents while studying nursing. Vera fled communist Czechoslovakia in 1968 and continues to live in Kingston, Canada.

Gerti Perutz Stalev was born in 1932 and lived with her Catholic mother in Prague during the German occupation. Her Jewish father, Leo Perutz, was arrested by the Nazis and in 1944 sent on the last transport to Auschwitz, where he was murdered. Gerti came to the US at age 18 to attend Indiana University and to pursue graduate work at Georgetown University. She had a career at the United Nations in New York. At times, she looked after me during the war. She now lives in Clayton, North Carolina.

I acknowledge the very supportive mentoring and teaching of several writers with whom I studied: Jimin Han and Gloria Hatrick at Sarah Lawrence College; Joan Potter at the Hudson Valley Writers Center; and from 2007 until 2018, Carol Henderson, author, teacher, editor and coach. Carol has a gift for listening carefully while guiding and encouraging writers as we seek to develop our craft.

No book would have been possible without the continuous support and special love from Michele Murdock, my partner and wife for the past 40 years. Michele is herself a published author. In *A Journey of Courage: The Amazing Story of Sister Dorothy Stang* she explores the courageous life of a martyr. Over the years Michele has read and reviewed several versions of my manuscript and has offered her wise counsel to improve the quality of my storytelling. Our son, Mike Stein, also a writer, has provided helpful commentary on various drafts. Mike, his wife Sarah, and their son Jackson have welcomed us to our new home in Washington, DC. Jackson is always fun to be with and has provided the kind of breaks from work writers periodically need.

This book took years to develop. It began the day a group of undergraduate students came to my office at William Paterson University in Wayne, N.J. I write about this pivotal experience in the preface. With colleagues Miryam Wahrman, Neil Kressel, David Shapiro, Carol Gruber, Vincent Parrillo and Fran Novick, I started teaching courses about genocide and the Holocaust and developed workshops for teachers, community members and organizations. At WPU, we were honored to receive funding for a number of years from Dr. Paul Winkler and the New Jersey Holocaust Commission. We developed many events, among them a community-wide presentation about Holocaust denial featuring historian Professor Deborah E. Lipstadt.

Michele and I moved to Chapel Hill, NC, in 2007 so that I could teach and do research at the Institute on Aging at the University of North Carolina.

In Chapel Hill, I met and worked with two second generation survivors, Sharon Halperin and Debbie Long, who developed the Holocaust Speakers Bureau of Chapel Hill and Durham (now the Center for Holocaust, Genocide, and Human Rights Education of North Carolina) dedicated to the teaching of the Holocaust. They inspired me to continue teaching today's students and adults. Thanks to Sharon and Debbie, I taught many elementary, middle and high school classes around the state, from Asheville to Wilmington to Elizabeth City to the Research Triangle. I learned from the students what they wanted to know about one of the darkest events of modern history, and their questions and curiosity have informed the way I wrote my story.

I was asked by Michael Abramson, chair of the North Carolina Council on the Holocaust, to serve as Holocaust Scholar from 2014 to 2016. With Lynda Moss and later Karen Klaich, I developed and delivered day-long workshops for teachers. I am grateful to a number of committed educators involved in these efforts to understand and teach about the Holocaust: Amy Clark, Lee Holder, Chrisy Horgan, Juanita Ray, Audrey Krakovitz, Cheryl Lange, Laurie Schaefer, MJ Limbo, Laurie Piner, Marianne Wason, Bonnie Hauser and Rose Mills.

Thanks also to our dear Chapel Hill friend Yvonne Trostli, who provided much support throughout the writing venture and who introduced me to Nora Gaskin Esthimer, a writer, editor and publisher of Lystra Books in Chapel Hill, NC. I am vey grateful to Nora, to copyeditor Karen N.V. Owen, to the Frogtown book designer, Beth Tashery Shannon, and to proofreader Rebecca Duncan.

While at the Institute on Aging from 2007 to 2016, I developed important friendships supportive of my writing venture. The Institute's Director, Victor Marshall, Ph.D. provided a stimulating academic home for writing. Chad Bryant, Ph.D., Professor of History at UNC-Chapel Hill, has examined the history of Eastern Europe, especially Czechoslovakia, and he graciously read the entire manuscript, offering important suggestions and factual corrections. William E. Leuchtenburg, Ph.D., William Rand Kenan Jr. Professor Emeritus of History at the UNC-Chapel Hill, demonstrated genuine interest in my writing project and has been a cheerful supporter of my efforts. Maureen Egen, the esteemed past publisher of the Time Warner Book Group, read an earlier version of the manuscript and provided valuable feedback. I am also grateful for the research assistance of Mira Markham, a graduate student in history at UNC, and the computer and photographic assistance of Ruth Briones.

I also thank other friends who read and provided feedback on the manuscript, including Judy Chatowsky, Elyse Crystal, Carol Dorsey, Karen Glodin, Mairead Maloney and Bill Powers. Special thanks to new Washington, DC friend Roxanne Walker, who is an extremely resourceful and committed photo researcher who helped organize the photos in my book.

I alone am responsible for any factual errors or omissions in the book. I welcome comments and responses from you, the readers.

Please reach me at aboysjourney@gmail.com.

Bibliography

Bauer, Yehuda. 2001. *A History of the Holocaust*. New York: Franklin Watts.

Brod, Petr, Kateřina Čapková and Mikal Frankl. 2010. "Czechoslovakia." *The YIVO Encyclopedia of Jews in Eastern Europe*. Retrieved May 5, 2015. (www.yivoencyclopedia.org/article.aspx/Czechoslovakia)

Bryant, Chad. 2007. *Prague in Black: Nazi Rule and Czech Nationalism*. Cambridge, MA: Harvard University Press.

Čapková, Kateřina. 2012. *Czechs, Germans, Jews? National Identity and the Jews of Bohemia*. New York: Berghahn Books.

Dean, Martin. 2001. *Collaboration in the Holocaust: Crimes of the Local Police in Belorussia and Ukraine 1941-44*. New York: Palgrave.

Dean, Martin. 2008. *Robbing the Jews: The Confiscation of Jewish Property in the Holocaust, 1933–1945*. New York: Cambridge University Press.

Demetz, Peter. 1997. *Prague in Black and Gold: Scenes in the Life of a European City*. New York: Hill and Wang.

Goodell, Stephen and Susan D. Bachrach. *Liberation 1945.* Washington, DC: United States Holocaust Memorial Museum, 1995.

Hajkova, Anna. 2014. "To Terezin and Back Again: Czech Jews and their Bonds of Belonging from Deportations to the Postwar," *Dapim: Studies of the Holocaust,* 28:1, 38-55.

Hajkova, Anna. 2016. "Women as Citizens in the Therese- instadt prisoner Community," *Online Encyclopedia of Mass Violence,* retrieved June 26, 2016. (www.sciencespo.fr/mass-violence-war-massacre-resis- tance/fr/node/3286)

Kovaly, Heda Margolius, trans. Helen Epstein. 2010. *Under a Cruel Star: A life in Prague 1941-1968.* Lexington MA: Plunkett Lake Press.

Kranzler, David. 1976. *Japanese, Nazi & Jews: The Jewish Refugee Community in Shanghai 1938-1945.* New York: Yeshiva University Press.

Lipstadt, Deborah. 1993. *Denying the Holocaust: The Growing Assault on Truth and Memory.* New York: Free Press.

Lipstadt, Deborah. 2019. *Antisemitism: Here and Now.* New York: Schoeken.

MacDonald, Callum and Jan Kaplan.1995. *Prague in the Shadow of the Swastika: A History of the German Occupa- tion 1939-1945.* Prague: Melantrich.

Rothkirchen, Livia. 2005. *The Jews of Bohemia and Moravia: Facing the Holocaust.* Lincoln: University of Nebraska Press and Yad Vashem.

Shermer, Michael and Alex Grobman. 2000. *Denying History: Who Says the Holocaust Never Happened and Why Do They Say It?* Berkeley, CA: University of California Press.

United States Holocaust Memorial Museum. Holocaust Encyclopedia, "Death Marches." Washington, DC. Retrieved Sept. 3, 2018. (encyclopedia.ushmm.org/content/en/article/death-marches-1)

United States Holocaust Memorial Museum. Holocaust Encyclopedia, "Theresteinstadt: Red Cross Visit." Washington, DC. Retrieved Sept. 15, 2018. (encyclopedia.ushmm.org/content/en/article/theresienstadt-red-cross-visit)

Wachsmann, Nikolaus. 2015. *KL: A History of the Nazi Concentration Camps.* New York: Farrar, Straus and Giroux.

Wistrich, Robert S. 2001. *Hitler and the Holocaust.* New York: Modern Library.

Zapruder, Alexandra. 2015. *Salvaged Pages: Young Writers' Diaries of the Holocaust.* New Haven: Yale University Press.

photograph by Gesche Wuerfel

Peter J. Stein is a retired sociology professor and author of books about families, work and careers, gender, aging and retirement. He is now engaged in Holocaust education for school children, college students and adults. For a number of years, he directed a Holocaust and Genocide Studies Center developing presentations and workshops for teachers, schools and community organizations. He lives in Washington, DC with his family, including his grandson.